THE PROJECT OF YOU, BEYOND HIGH SCHOOL

MASTER THE 5 KEY SKILLS FOR YOUR FUTURE SUCCESS

BRENDA JO MARCH

DEDICATION

For Jim, My Husband and Best Friend
Your Constant Love and Support make anything possible.

For Kelsey, Lindsay and Dan, My three Amazing HHSS children
Your Beauty, Brilliance and Compassion are a constant inspiration to me

CONTENTS

A NOTE TO PARENTS
AND GUARDIANS:

FOR PARENTS AND guardians of students reading this book, as a parent of three young adults myself, it's hard to step back and allow them to find their way. In fact, I don't think it's necessary to completely step back but I do believe your students have to learn to ask and trust others for help. That is part of the growth and exploration they need to become HHSS: Happy, Healthy and Self-Supporting. But in many cases, they need a guidebook, course or project plan to get started. The goal of this book is to help them develop their own plan and learn to execute it independently.

None of us have all the answers but we do know we want more for our children. We hear all the statistics regarding lack of jobs and college debt. In addition, studies show that 70% of the US workforce is disengaged and unhappy in their positions. This is not the first H— happy— or what we want for our students. How can we help our students become empowered? We need to let them figure it all out on their own and feel confident by researching, creating and executing their plan. The big BUT is that it's not incredibly easy to seek out and find this information and it's not always a part of their high school or college curriculum. There is an abundance of information and they need to sort through and decide what information is valid. Developing connections with reliable, trusted sources of information is crucial for their success. Given many students' school and extracurricular schedules, time is often not allotted as a part of their academic studies to do the research and digging deeper to get them connected to an idea or concept of who they are and who they can be if they explore and gain experience.

We all know this is intense inner work that requires insight and digging deep. Encourage your students to share what they are discovering with you but also encourage the research and exploration and experiential learning that is key to success. Empower your students by allowing them to find their own way rather than telling them what to do. Students are ready for this path at varying times.

When do you know a student is ready? They are ready when they accept offers for help or ask for help or seek out opportunities to make it happen. If you want to help them be ready sooner, offer opportunities for college visits, job shadowing, volunteering, and other experiential learning whenever possible. You can also hire a coach or educational consultant or sign them up for a career exploration workshop.

Seeds have to be planted and ideas have to be washed over them to make the transition from being a high school student to beyond. Parents, guardians, teachers, coaches, and mentors have to support and help students feel comfortable marching forward on their own. Do not do the work for them but empower them to begin exploring early. They may not understand that a Beyond High School plan can involve making a potential $200K investment decision. Whether or not they earn a bachelor's degree can make a difference of $1 million lifetime earning potential. Many students benefit from an impartial third party so consider hiring a coach, mentor or educational consultant anytime from 8th to 12th grade.

As a parent or guardian, insist on documentation for college visits. I have a college or technical school visit checklist that your student can download from my website. Ask your students to give you progress updates as they make their *Project of You Plan*. Give them encouragement and be open to their possibilities and share ideas and connections. Help your students connect with like-minded adults in areas of interest for them. Learning to network is a skill that requires practice and repetition. Truly understanding the possibilities in a specific industry or field requires research and experience, what I refer to as "digging deeper." You may not have to be the one to help them rule in or rule out a potential career path. With enough information and experience, your students will make these choices independently.

For myself as a parent, what I want most for my children is for them to be happy and healthy and self-sufficient or supporting - HHSS. Yes in some ways I want them to have a better life than I did but that is so open to interpretation that it is difficult to make 100% clear, because what my children define as happy and healthy and self-supporting may be somewhat different than my definition. To break it down even further, we could consider the following as reasonable definitions.

Happy: feeling pleasure, satisfied, fortunate.

Healthy: fit, well, psychologically sound, in good condition, strong, vigorous.

Self-Supporting: independent, autonomous, opposite of dependent.

Supporting is a relative term, because everyone has differing definitions of what they need financially to survive. For me, self-supporting means that I no longer need to subsidize them. I can enjoy being generous and buying them gifts if I choose, but I no longer have to pay their day-to-day living expenses.

Reviewing these definitions, I can truly say that this is enough for me as a parent. I am fortunate that each of my children is currently happy, healthy and self –supporting; perhaps not in the style that they have grown accustomed to, as they are early in their career path. But I am not worried about them being able to support themselves. They have all held jobs and been successful, and I am confident that they have the skills needed to find and be successful in a career as needed in their lives. My greatest hope for my children and any student is this: what they choose to do as a profession can provide enough financially at any given point in time for them to be comfortable, and that they will learn to live within their means. I also wish for them to feel happy, fulfilled and passionate about either what they do as a career or in their personal lives as a volunteer, or family member or member of a group. If they could be excited about all areas of their lives that would be perfect but if not, I hope that they can focus on the good things in their life and not let the difficulties bring them down. We all need to learn to be happy and healthy and self-supporting. As the Dalai Lama states in his book, *The Art of Happiness*, "A tree with strong roots can withstand the most violent storm, but the tree can't grow roots just as the storm appears on the horizon." Those necessary roots need to be consistently groomed both in our academic mind and outward abilities as well as in our inner mind and soul. We need to cultivate both. Sir Ken Robinson, an author, speaker and international advisor on education states: "we tend to use a manufacturing model in education and we need to switch to an agricultural model where we consider the needs of each student."

But remember - it's all up to them. You can help guide them and continue to be their biggest fans and advocates, but give them the space to develop their own "The Project of You, Beyond High School" plan. If it's their plan, it means they have bought into it and will be more likely to complete it.

The greatest gift a parent can give a child

is the ability to become independently happy.

And the greatest gift a child can give a parent is exercising

that ability.

BEFORE YOU BEGIN:

You are about to begin the Project of You journey to make your unique plan for your next steps beyond high school. You will be introduced to new key skills for success that require your full focus to make a difference in your future. The time you will spend is an investment in your future success.

Why am I the one to write this book? I work with people your age all the time. I also work with individual professionals and organizations and know how these success skills have helped them grow. Why not start mastering these skills earlier?

I spent 25-plus years in business working as a Project Manager or managing groups of Project Managers. I discovered every project starts with wanting to make something or achieve an outcome and then working backward building the plan. To be successful in the Project of You, you will decide how to "define you beyond high school." Then you will work backwards developing all the tasks you need to do to reach your unique desired outcome. This project will require completing the readings and exercises in five key personal success skills to develop your individual outcome. Once you know your targeted outcome based on your individual interests, strengths and passions, you can develop a plan for your Project of You Beyond High School.

The laser focus exercise below is how I start every session with clients in person or group coaching settings. My clients have shared that it helps them focus. If you are reading this book to consider The Project of You, Life Beyond High School, it is important to your future success and will require your laser focus - no multi-tasking.

Clearing your brain to make space for new ideas, thoughts, and energies will give your brain a laser focus and is worth the few minutes the exercise will require. I would also suggest that if you put the book down mid-read, do this laser focus exercise again before going back to reading more.

Take a moment before you read the next line to take three deep breaths and clear your mind and let go of any nagging thoughts that you may have.

If you need to send yourself a text or add the tasks swirling around in your head to your to-do list on your computer or journal or wherever you keep your pressing tasks, **do that now and get it on paper and out of your thoughts.**

Next, unless you have: a family member on a transplant list or

you are bleeding profusely or you are an emergency response person,

close out your email,

put your laptop or iPad in sleep mode,

turn off your cell phone and

focus on just this information for the moment. It will mean more later.

Now turn the page and get started learning what you can do for yourself to guarantee your future success!

WHAT IS THE MOST IMPORTANT PROJECT YOU WILL EVER WORK ON?

THE PROJECT OF You is the most important project you will ever work on. This is because it will provide you a concrete plan for beyond high school so you can easily choose the best path for your future. There are numerous options for you beyond high school; connecting to the right plan for you will require some effort. You have done many projects throughout your school career so you know that to plan a project you have to be clear on the outcome.

The goal of this book is to provide you opportunities to spend small amounts of time in regular intervals to decide on the perfect path for you. By completing the readings and exercises in this book, you will:

- learn to budget time for your exploration;
- increase your self-awareness about your vision for your future;
- find your "why" and connection to the world beyond high school;
- improve your personal communication skills;
- acknowledge your core values to help you make future choices; and
- begin developing ideas around the direction in which you want to head as an adult.

Colleges, universities, career training programs, and alternative beyond high school programs, all require a huge investment of your time. If you choose college as your initial next step, it takes at least four years to complete an undergraduate degree. In addition, it's a huge investment of your money or possibly other adults' money such as your parents or guardians or scholarship providers. Or you may decide to take out student loans and those debts can take a long time to pay back. Any beyond high school choice will require you to invest your time and money. You want to be sure you are investing in the right place for you.

Marching forward beyond high school requires this process to become self-aware and find your direction to make a plan for the best path for you.

Why invest the time and money without a clear path to follow?

As a parent of three young adults, I watched them sometimes struggle to define their plan. As their parent, I wanted to help in any way I could, including trying to make their plan for them. Perhaps your parents have done the same? It's only because we care so much and at one point it was our job to take care of everything for you. But a while back, I was given some wise advice by a colleague of mine. He said to me, "You can't project manage your kids." I realized he was right, but I also realized that they could learn to project manage themselves if someone taught them how. It's not hard, but it is an important process that you need to go through to find the right path for you. You can create your *Project of You Plan* and feel ready too.

Many parents or other adult advisors may try to "guide" you in your plan. Take any opportunities for advice and guidance and consider what you learn in these moments.

Some people may feel they know you better than you know yourself -prove them wrong. You know what's best for you.

You want to know yourself better than anyone else. Discover who you are and what you want. When you choose your path, share it with confidence. Developing your own personal plan is not always a course offered in your school, but now you have an opportunity to learn how to make your own *Project of You Plan*.

Do you know what next steps you want to take to reach your goals?

You will wear many hats, but will you choose your hats or let someone else make those choices for you?

By reading this book and understanding the five key success skills and doing the exercises, you will make the most of your personal time and money investment choices for beyond high school.

Before now, as a student, what has been expected of you has been fairly clear and predictable. During your school career, you attend classes on a planned schedule and typically move ahead based on meeting progress requirements that your teachers define. In some cases, parents and other experts are also involved in deciding your progress and choosing classes and levels for you. In the majority of cases, you move to the next grade without a lot of planning or preparation. If you do what is expected of you, you advance.

In most elementary schools, your classes were planned for you based on your school curriculum and your abilities. When you moved on to middle school, you began to have choices dependent on your school.

In high school, you select your classes. This could be based on your interest level, your abilities, or what your guidance counselor or parents and guardians or other experts recommend, or what you believe you want to do beyond high school. If you know you are going to college or a technical school or stepping into a career, your choices will need to be based on the specific requirements for each of those possibilities. During your K–12 school years, your teachers and parents and guardians help keep you accountable with grades and homework assignments to make sure you are successful and move ahead. During middle school and high school, you want to develop personal accountability to be prepared for life beyond high school.

From now on, if you choose college there will also be required general education credits as well as specific required classes for your major. Many choices are up to you but there are still many requirements that you must complete. Being aware of the requirements is a key to success. Making the most of your general education courses and electives is another key. You may have heard the story, but Steve Jobs took a calligraphy course as an elective because it fascinated him, not because it was required or because someone recommended it to him. Here is a quote from Steve Jobs Stanford Commencement speech:

"I decided to take a calligraphy class . I learned about serif and sans-serif typefaces, about varying the space between different letter combinations, about what makes great typography great. It was beautiful. Historical. Artistically subtle in a way that science can't capture. And I found it fascinating. None of this had any hope of any practical application in my life. But 10 years later, when we were designing the first Macintosh computer, it all came back to me. And we designed it all into the Mac. It was the first computer with beautiful typography. If I had never dropped in on that single course in college, the Mac would never have multiple typefaces or proportionally spaced fonts. And since Windows just copied the Mac, it's likely that no personal computer would have them. Keep learning and experiencing new things; you never know how or when it may make an impact in the future."

I fully agree with Steve's words - allow yourself to be open to new possibilities.

If college is not in your future plans, what do you need for success in your plan? Perhaps you are planning to go to a technical school and learn a trade; what will that require? Or maybe you are planning to become a part of the family business or transition into another business that interests you? Some students choose to do a GAP year and learn more about themselves before going to college or starting a career; is that right for you? What will you need to add to your *Project of You Plan* to be successful in your chosen path beyond high school?

These are the types of questions you will be able to answer after completing the Project of You.

You will discover this personal reality in your own way. There is a pivotal time transitioning from childhood to adulthood, when you will recognize that who you become and what you do with your life is your decision and no one else's. You have the ability to make your own choices. You will be your own advocate. You will ask for help if you need it. You will be the superhero of your own life.

If you learn nothing else from this book, here is the most important message:

It's all up to you!

You can decide whether or not you want to go to college.

You can decide whether or not to do a GAP year.

You can decide on a college major.

You can decide to take a year off and gain work experience.

You can decide to start your own business.

You can decide to work and take courses online.

You can decide to go to college part time initially and do further career exploration.

You can decide whether or not to take on college debt and your personal debt limit.

Owning the plan and following through with it - that part is fully up to you! No one else can make these decisions for you. The adults with the money, such as parents and guardians, mentors, and scholarship providers will likely have a big influence in most cases, especially in relation to the financial aspects of your decision. If they are helping you pay for college or a gap year or technical school, then it's only fair to work collaboratively with them as they are making an investment in you and your future. No matter what, do your research and make a plan and march forward into your future success!

There are many options to take a step in the right direction planning your future by hiring a coach or mentor or educational consultant or talking to your parents or guardians or other adults you trust. Or do all of these things. These are all good options but you can also make a great plan on your own by learning the five key skills for success in this book.

There are lots of people and resources and guidance available for you to get where you want to go. There are many people to help you and I have listed some within this book. But none of them have your personal Project of You perspective of the outcome you want to achieve. Remember, the choices and decisions and commitments are yours to make.

Commit, go all in for yourself, imagine where you want to be and develop your personal plan to make it happen. That is my hope for you.

You owe it to yourself to know yourself!

You have to know what you want before you can ask for it or go find it or create it.

~ Brenda Jo March

YOUR CONCERNS BEYOND HIGH SCHOOL

YOU MAY HAVE a clear idea of your plan beyond high school or you may have some questions or fears. Sometimes it's hard to figure out on your own what's holding you back. This is true at any age but deciding what's next beyond high school is a huge decision. I've shared an example below to give you a sense of how one young woman felt and how she marched forward. By the way, since my last name is March, I have named my business March Forward Consulting, and your plan will enable you to march forward towards your future success!

I knew a young woman who wasn't getting her college applications done. She couldn't seem to get motivated to do them and couldn't figure out what was holding her back. I coached her and as we discussed why she was working with me, we began to uncover her fears and blocks and discovered some interesting facts.

Kate initially said she had no idea what she wanted to do and wasn't sure she wanted to go to college. Kate's heart and mind were open to the opportunity to try and uncover her path. She was totally present during our meetings but it was clear there were fears in her mind. At first, she didn't fully understand her fears and wasn't able to express her feelings.

Kate is a beautiful young woman who was academically successful, involved in various extracurricular activities, and held a part time job as well. Yet she was uncertain if she wanted to go to college, what to major in or if she would be successful. Why? That was a question for us to solve together. Kate and I spent additional sessions together reviewed her assessments and progress reports, and she began to share more and dig deeper.

She had three prominent fears:

1. *Could she get into a "well known and recognized school" with her current grades and SAT scores? Kate referred to this as a "good" school. She was concerned about other people's perception of the schools that would be on her list of options. Many students I have met have the perception that a name brand is key in choosing a college? Brand recognition is important in marketing.* Yet a Ferrari for $295,000 and a Scion for $15,000 can both take you where you want to go.

2. *She was worried because she wasn't doing well in some of her A/P classes, specifically A/P science classes. She had always been a strong student and her grades had dropped in her A/P classes. Perhaps the A/P label had frightened her. If she believed that it would be too hard for her, it could be. As it does for many students, it may have "psyched her out". But a C in an A/P class is the same as a B in a regular class and might better prepare her for college level classes.*

3. *Kate had been told by many people that she should be a nurse because of her extreme sense of responsibility, compassion, desire to help others, and kindness. She wasn't sure if that was truly what she wanted to do. And given her struggle in science classes, she didn't perceive it as an option. That was a decision she could make through exploration, experience and increasing her self- awareness.*

As we talked further, her fears about getting into her definition of a "good" school were mainly because she didn't want her parents to be embarrassed by her college choice options. She wanted them to be proud to tell everyone else where she was going to college. Other friends at school who were currently more successful academically were applying to schools that were considered more prestigious and "hard to get into", and she knew that was not likely to be her path. Kate also had an older sister who was stronger academically and currently attended a "prestigious" college.

We began exploring what she felt her parents' perception of her was. Did she think her parents were proud of her? Could she talk to her parents about how she was feeling? Are grades and test scores really the measure of success? Who do you think is successful now? Are they always the people who were straight A students in high school classes?

Kate left with her homework and came back with answers to some of these questions. And when she did come back with her inquiries completed, she was surprised at what she had discovered. Many people that she considered successful were not straight A students from prestigious colleges. Perhaps that is not the only thing that matters.

She also discussed with her parents their feelings about her college options and alleviated that issue from her heart and mind. Her parents said they wouldn't be embarrassed by any of her choices. They believed she would be successful no matter what she chose to do because of her many wonderful qualities and strong skills. Her personal research along with her uncomfortable but important conversations with her parents relieved her first block.

We began zeroing in on her choices and how she could "find her connection". She wasn't certain she wanted to be a nurse but hadn't totally ruled out the possibility. She agreed to set up a job shadow to truly gain exposure into the daily life of a nurse. When she came back for her next session, she had completed the job shadow and realized that she was 100% energized about the possibility of being a nurse. In talking to several of the nurses that she met while job shadowing, she learned that her compassionate, kind nature combined with her quick mind would definitely assist her in being a great nurse.

Kate also learned more about her concerns regarding her grades. She talked about whether or not every "now expert" nurse had been

15

a straight A, A/P science student in high school. She did her own informal survey and discovered that only 2 out of 5 successful nurses she had met had taken A/P science classes in high school. She shared her fear regarding her struggle with her A/P science classes with some of the nurses. These experienced nurses could see that she had the desire and heart to be a nurse and had the potential to successfully complete the academic work. They told her to not worry about her grades. Her grades weren't bad. It was just her perception. Her job shadowing and follow up discussions had alleviated her other fears and blocks.

Now it was time to get busy filling out her applications and making plans for her future! Interestingly, after she made her decision to head down the path as a nurse, began applying to colleges that fit her profile, and focused on her strengths rather than her weaknesses, her grades in her A/P classes also improved. I believe this is because she found her connection! Reading this book will also help you discover your connection and develop the best plan for you.

Having a plan and always looking for positive angles can change your attitude. Watch this video by searching for:

Zig Ziglar - Attitude Makes All The Difference

Your attitude about Your *Project of You Plan* can make all the difference in YOUR future success beyond high school.

DON'T LET FEAR STOP YOU
FROM EXPLORING

AS YOU CAN see from Kate's story, fear can overwhelm you and stop you from marching forward. The biggest stumbling block I find teenagers as well as adults have is FEAR. To complete the exercises and readings in this book, you will explore new ideas and make new choices; don't let fear stop you!.

What is FEAR? Fear is defined as an unpleasant emotion based on worry or the belief there is danger. When a person is doing something new, it is an unknown so it's easy to believe there could be danger. An acronym for

FEAR is False Expectations Appearing Real,

and many people have a natural tendency to let those false expectations create worry and stress and in some cases stop them from marching forward. How do these fears develop? Are our fears something we are born with?

"Human beings are born with just two basic fears. One is the fear of loud noises. The other is the fear of falling. All other fears must be learned."

~ Ronald Rood

What fears have you learned?

The fear of:

- choosing the wrong major,
- not being ready for college,
- college debt,
- choosing an alternate path,
- not finding your true connection/purpose, or
- asking for what you truly want!

Many students feel fear of their future and the unknown beyond high school. It makes sense to be apprehensive. High school tends to be predictable; beyond high school is an open book with many questions. There are many choices and the more you can release your fears, the more experiences you will be able to enjoy and gain knowledge to assist you in developing your plan.

The key to releasing fears is to acknowledge them and then recognize why they are not true - why they are false expectations appearing real. Your fears live only in your brain but it is a struggle that all people have to learn to overcome. Write your fears down and share them with a trusted friend or advisor. You can then address whether or not they are real or false expectations. Kate's story earlier in the book gave several examples of how Kate recognized and documented her fears and then was able to overcome them by addressing them one by one. For each of her three initial fears, she was able to actually find a way to make her fears an opportunity. By acknowledging her fears and addressing them, she learned more about who she was, how her parents felt about her, what she wanted to do with her future, and what she needed to succeed.

After Kate had all her applications for school done and was accepted to her first choice college, she was again feeling a new fear. Kate and I met and brainstormed what was worrying her. She was afraid of heading into unknown territory - of going to college. Kate used the FEAR worksheet and again overcame her fear.

Kate's example FEAR worksheet:

What is your FEAR? *I am afraid of going to college. I might not be comfortable and might not be successful.*

What is your FEAR based on? *Lack of knowing what to expect and thinking I could fail socially and academically.*

Why do you feel this way? *Because other people I have known have not been successful in college.*

Is this fear true for you? *Maybe? I don't know what to expect.*

What questions can you answer for yourself to make your fear an opportunity?

How can I learn more about what to expect in college?

Why would I not be successful?

Do I want a college degree enough to give it my best?

What lessons can I learn from the people I know who weren't successful?

What lessons can I learn from people who have been successful?

Have you ever experienced this same type of fear in the past? When? *Yes, when I started my part time job at Panera.*

If yes to # 6, how did you overcome it then? *I made sure I was as prepared as possible, took a deep breath, told myself I would be fine and can do anything, and went for it.*

What can you learn about yourself from your past fears and successes? *My fears and worrying were either falsely predicting my outcome or sabotaging myself and were a waste of my brain energy.*

What can you do to overcome fears in the future? *Stop and recognize what my fears are and why they are false expectations appearing real.*

So if you are experiencing fears through any of the exercises in this book, download the **My Fear Worksheet** from my website: www. marchforwardconsulting.com or utilize the **My Fear Worksheet** in The Project of You workbook and consider your past.

Think back to other times when you were afraid in your past, perhaps:

- when you left elementary school for middle school, or

- when you tried out for a theatre group, or

- when you moved from middle school to high school, or

- when your parent or guardian moved to a new job so you went to a new school, or

- when you went to sleep away camp for the first time,

- when you accepted a part time job as a lifeguard, or

- any other new experience that seemed scary at first.

In each of those cases, you took a deep breath and faced your fear and marched forward. Whether or not you were successful in past endeavors, each experience provided a learning opportunity. You learned more about yourself, what you can do, what you like, and whether or not being fearful changed the outcome.

How can you unlearn and conquer your fears?

You can conquer your fears by facing them head on, admitting you have them and then asking yourself why? Are your fears justified? Do you have a reason to believe that you are in danger? If there is a true danger, then stop but if your fears are false expectations appearing real, then push yourself beyond your comfort zone and march forward.

You can do the same thing with your Beyond High School plan if you have given it the time and energy it deserves, don't be afraid.

In addition to our fears of what to expect beyond high school, many students are afraid:

- to be authentic and share your differences,
- to admit what they want because it might not be what is recommended or expected,
- to look inside themselves,
- to ask for what they want,
- of the answer they will get when asking someone for help,
- to admit that they want or need help.

Remember, your FEAR can be your own worst enemy.

Why do many come to believe that the others make all the rules and live in fear of questioning the status quo? Perhaps we are educated to be conformists - to not question authority. Seth Godin shares in, "Stop Stealing Dreams", "Given that the assigned output of school is compliant citizens, the shortcut for achieving this output was fear. If your intentions are fueled by true individual passion they can overcome your amygdala, lizard brain and the fears within it. But the fear mindset does serve us at times; it stops us from making hasty, uninformed decisions. "

You get what you expect in life; so what if you expect your new experience to be wonderful? Do not let fear stop you. It can be FEAR of the unknown or FEAR of making the wrong choice or FEAR of not being good enough but all fear has the same effect. Fear can overwhelm and stop you from marching forward with the belief that you deserve the best and can achieve it if you try. Whatever fears you have, try the fear worksheet and find a way to turn your fears into opportunities.

Remember:

> ***Any fear that you have learned can be unlearned!***
> ***~Brenda Jo March***

As you move into adulthood, you may believe it is all up to you and it is. But never be afraid to ask for help, we are all put here on this earth to help each other. Most adults will feel honored if you request their help. What is the worst that can happen if you ask someone for help? The worst possible answer is they say no.

Are you afraid of getting a NO?

Do you not ask for help because you think the answer will be no?

But consider what the answer is if you don't ask.

If you don't ask, the answer will always be a NO. ~ Nora Roberts

No can be a strong word when it comes to determining your choices in life. It gives you clarity. Once you get a No you can make a decision, move forward, and make a new plan.

If you get a yes that's great too, if what you asked for is what you really wanted.

The only really bad word to be given as an answer is maybe; it's not an answer and you are left still wondering where you stand - not a good feeling.

Why is "maybe" a bad word? Perhaps when you ask your parents to buy you a car, they say maybe. If they said yes, you might ask when? But you would be relaxed and happy knowing you would be getting a car. If they said no, you would know you better get a job and start saving if you want a car. But if they say maybe, you don't know where you stand or if you have to make a new plan and when. The word "maybe" does not give you clarity to be able to know your next move.

In some cases perhaps you are saying maybe to yourself. Let me give you an example.

I have met many high school students who aren't sure they want to go to college. They live in the land of maybe and because it's a maybe, they don't do the research needed to make a decision. In fact, they don't make any decisions. They tell themselves they are thinking about it, and some are thinking about it, but thinking isn't doing. Thinking about an idea is different than actual strategy and execution. The goal of The Project of You Plan is to not only think about what you want to do but also begin the actual strategy and execution of developing your individual plan. The students who decide they don't want to go to college immediately know they need an alternate plan and so they begin researching and making a plan for either a GAP year or a technical school or career alternative that fits a high school graduate. The students who know they do want to go to college begin exploring potential college and major choices and taking the next steps needed and doing that exploration. If you don't pick one path or the other, you aren't going anywhere. If you are unsure, pick one path and research it. You can always change your mind but don't just think about it - unless thinking about it includes actually exploring alternatives for one choice or the other or both.

YOUR QUESTIONS

I'M GOING TO ask you a series of questions to see how prepared you are to stand up for yourself. How would you answer these questions now?

1. Who am I?

2. What do I want?

3. Where am I going?

4. How do I get there?

You probably have answers to some or all of these questions but if not, don't worry. By the end of this book and by completing Your *Project of You Plan*, you will have answers and a plan. I have worked with many people of all ages in many capacities over the years as a coach, consultant, and even as a parent, and many people aren't able to answer these questions beyond this moment. And I agree with "living in the moment" but making a plan and setting goals is also important. Give yourself the time, energy and focus to understand the five key success skills. Then you will be able to answer these questions and have a plan for your next step beyond high school. And as time goes by, if you need to change your path, you will know the steps to take to update your *Project of You Plan* and march forward in a new direction. The key is to remember that you are the only one who can answer these questions for yourself. Don't think that anyone else can answer these questions for you. These are your questions to ponder and make choices for your future.

Many people let others tell them what they should do and follow them down a path that appears to make sense for them. Letting others control your life is how you start out as young children. Now it's important to take potential suggestions and advice from others only if it fits what you want. It's when you begin to understand yourselves and recognize you can make your choices that the game changes. And this is where you want to be to make the transition from childhood to adulthood.

Let me give you an example from my own life when I was in high school to help you understand. You may become passionate about something based on a life experience such as I did.

I had a friend who was suffering from depression and was prescribed Valium.

I didn't think this was a good treatment. Why? My friend seemed to be worse on the Valium, spending long periods of time in bed. She seemed to be more lethargic and uninterested in life than before she was treated. I didn't believe this was right; I expected the medication to help her feel better not worse. I felt passionate that medication was not the answer in her case.

I assumed there were many others like her so I decided to become a psychiatrist and try to change this process. I couldn't do anything to help my friend at the time but I believed when I became a psychiatrist, I wouldn't treat people with medication. Right then and there I decided on this plan without doing any additional research. What I didn't comprehend at that point in time is that prescribing medications is the reason most people go to a psychiatrist. If I didn't believe medication was the answer, why choose that career path? And what I didn't understand at that point in my life is that some people do need medications for mental illnesses and those people are helped by those medications. My friend's parents eventually weaned her off the medication, and found her a counselor who was able to help her utilizing counseling and other alternative techniques. It was great to see her begin to improve.

As you can see, I didn't do any true career exploration. I simply decided based on one example and a wrong I believed that wanted to right. I honestly thought that by majoring in psychology, I could influence people not to solve depression with medication. I wish I had understood when I was in high school that it wasn't about my jumping through hoops just because that is what you are supposed to do next. I went to college because it was what you were supposed to do. I also wanted people to find ways to deal with their problems beyond using medications. I didn't understand at that point in my life that some people need and are helped by use of medication for psychiatric illnesses.

But I wasn't aware that I would need to at least get my Master's degree to actually make what I now feel is a livable wage with a psychology degree working within the psychology field. Given that I had to pay my own way through college and take out loans, once I graduated, the thought of additional schooling and additional debt was not my first choice. Because I hadn't made a Project of You Plan for myself, I didn't fully understand what I was doing or why I was doing it or where it would eventually take me. I had a thought but not a true plan.

If you complete your *Project of You Plan* now, you'll be ready for whatever path you choose! Some people spend their entire lives never reaching this place where they have a plan that connects them to their passions and strengths and their "why". If your high school, offers a course to help you decide who you are, your strengths, your possibilities, and what you want out of life, I strongly urge you to take it. If not, take the time and energy to read this book or take a course, to connect you to who you want to be and where you want to go before leaving high school.

Getting to know yourself and how you can potentially share your unique genius with the world is a gift. One I hope that you give yourself!

Wherever you are now in this world, is up to only one person - you!

You are the most important project you will ever work on so let's get down to tactics!

YOUR FIVE KEY SKILLS FOR SUCCESS

THERE ARE FIVE overarching key skills for success that you need to master to create your *Project of You Plan*. These five key skills for success will help you be stronger and clearer throughout your life. They are based on my years of training, research and experience as a consultant, coach and mentor. Finding clarity in each of these areas allows you to easily make the choices you need beyond high school. The more you learn about yourself, the simpler it will be for you to choose a direction, be adaptable and communicate your personal needs. Mastering the five key skills for success will make it easy to march forward on your path. Or if in the future you decide to change your path, you can use these same five keys for success and exercises to update your *Project of You Plan*. Each of these five key skills for success is an important part of your unique plan to choose your next step beyond high school.

As you are learning about various aspects of each of these key skills for success, you will be asked to complete various exercises. Each of these exercises will provide you with additional insights into the best path for you.

Stay organized throughout the process; each exercise is one part of a big puzzle. Decide to either start a file online on your computer or some other electronic device and maintain your notes electronically or designate a notebook or folder to keep all of your hardcopy

Project of You materials in one place. Until you can connect all your dots, each dot is important.

Two important notes:

1. Given the advances in technology, you have a unique opportunity to build on what you learn from this project. In the past many people have maintained diaries or hard copy journals or notebooks. If you are a person who likes paper, that's fine but you can also keep an online version that you can reference and easily add to in the future. If you prefer working on paper, scan your documents as you complete them and add them to your file. You are learning more about you through this process and while your outer world is constantly changing, who you are as a person inside is a constant. You may feel the need to go back and reference these materials again two years or twenty years from now.

2. While this is a great guide to create your *Project of You Plan* for beyond high school, there is a benefit to working with a coach or consultant. Coaches and consultants are not only for adults; many high school students also benefit by working with a coach. When I work with clients, many new ideas and thoughts are uncovered organically as a part of the coaching process. As you may know, often times one question leads to another, and this type of collaboration often leads to many great insights and ideas. In addition, working with an objective adult who doesn't have a biased concept of who you are from past experience always provides a fresh perspective. So you may want to enhance your experience by engaging a coach, consultant or mentor.

Your investment of your energy and time to explore each key skill for success in relation to you will give you the clarity and confidence needed to march forward beyond high school successfully. Make the time for you and invest in you!

1. **Time** – Give yourselves the time to develop and execute a plan to move ahead based solely on your unique genius. Planning also requires time for research and exploration; it's not all on an easily documented menu because what you do is unique to you only.

2. **Self- awareness** – Search inside yourself to understand how you feel and why you feel that way in any given situation. Develop a strong sense of self to present your best and authentic self as you march forward and make connections to develop your unique Project of You plan. Learn to seek answers within you, not to seek answers about who you are from the outside world.

3. **Connection** – Now that you have increased your self – awareness, discover your "why" and find the types of people and activities that are a strong, positive connection for you uniquely, not based on pleasing someone else. Research potential paths for your unique *Project of You Plan*. Learn how to seek assistance, answers, and change within your small community and in the bigger outside world.

4. **Communication skills** – Now that you know what you want, learning how to ask for and get what you want is the next step. This becomes easier after understanding your time, self-awareness and connection key skills for success. Learning to communicate your true self and be authentic requires releasing your "learned" fears.

5. **Values clarification** – Understanding what values are your personal highest priorities allow you to clearly make difficult choices. When you go against your values, you won't feel right about it in your heart or gut. If you know your values and are true to your values, it all feels right and you have clarity for difficult decisions.

Most any personal struggle can be categorized within one of these five key skills. If you learn to effectively use each of these key skills, and become strong and clear in relation to all five, you will have the ability to achieve your goals and live a positive, energetic, productive life. You will become my favorite outcome for anyone's *Project of You Plan*: HHSS – Happy, Healthy and Self-supporting.

DO YOU LIKE GREEN
EGGS AND HAM?

HAVE YOU READ Dr. Suess' book: *Green Eggs and Ham*? Perhaps you read it as a child. The main character does everything in his power to avoid trying "Green Eggs and Ham" because he is certain without trying them that he hates them. As the book continues he is urged over and over again to try Green eggs and ham, and he keeps saying NO. Finally, one day he is convinced to try them. Surprise (spoiler alert for those who don't know the ending), he finds out that he likes Green eggs and ham. And now he wants to eat them any chance he gets.

In a similar way, you now have to discover more about you and researching your potential interest areas to make a conscious choice about your future. Don't let discovering who you are and developing your *Project of You Plan* overwhelm you anymore than trying new foods. It's that easy.

Think about it. Do you realize how much time and energy has been spent in your life learning what foods you love to eat? Most people eat three meals a day and occasional snacks. Each time you eat something, you are making a conscious choice of what you want. In most cases, it's based on your past experience of having that food or your curiosity and desire to try something new. Think back and consider how much time you have spent, without knowing it, learning about and discovering new foods. And how you have tasted and tested and decided what works for you.

What you like to eat and what is good for your unique DNA is just one facet of who you are and generally you have researched, taste-tested, and decided what you like to give you freedom and find happiness. You have spent a ton of time unconsciously learning, exploring and developing your own personal and unique food choices and the options are endless. Your life is like a big buffet and you have decided which items are your favorites.

Think of your life and the choices that you make the way you choose your next meal. Whether you are scanning a printed menu or walking through a self -service restaurant line, you are choosing options based on what you know about yourself.

There are foods:

- you love and you know that because you have tried them.

- you don't enjoy eating but you would likely eat them if they were the only things being served.

- you hate and may not eat if even if you are hungry.

- you are allergic to and they are dangerous for you to eat.

- you like but they don't make you feel well.

- you have read about and always wanted to try.

You may be a person who is always willing to try new foods. You can take the same attitude towards your *Project of You Plan* development. Picking new items from the buffet to try may be outside of your current comfort zone but the more foods you are willing to try, the more interesting your life will be. As the saying goes, "Variety is the spice of life". While choosing your path may seem extremely different than learning what you love to eat, it's similar in that you can stay in the safe zone, eat what you know, and not try new things or be curious and experiment.

There are many options for things to do to both support yourself and "fulfill" yourself beyond the structure of high school. It's up to you to develop your personal menu with you as your own personal menu planner. Perhaps while in high school, breakfast and dinner were whatever was being served where you grew up. Lunch was a selection from the school cafeteria or what you packed from home. Now you may have favorites on the menus at Chipotle or Panera or many other chains or local eateries. You may have begun trying foods from various cultures other than your native culture.

As an adult, you have the freedom to choose when, what, where and how you will eat to please and maintain your unique body. In addition, as an adult you also begin to have more choices around:

- the classes you choose to take,

- the experiences that you choose to find for yourself,

- the way you schedule and plan your time,

- what you eat,

- when you sleep,

- whether or not you go to class, and

most of all, what you make of the time and energy and genius that is you!

So take this project seriously and be open to new things, just as you likely are with trying new foods.

Trying something and realizing you don't like it is better than never trying it.

Think about an experience when someone wanted you to try something and you said no but later learned you liked it? When your friends invited you for sushi, or something they would feature on bizarre foods and you said no. But when you finally agreed to try it, you loved it.

Be open to trying new things and exploring all possibilities as you march forward to develop your *Project of You Plan*. There are so many new opportunities in high school to learn more about you and discover possible career paths.

You can:

- join a new club,
- try a new sport,
- start a new habit,
- take an interesting elective,
- go on a job shadow,
- find an internship, or

whatever you choose, the possibilities are numerous.

Why waste time saying you don't like something you never tried like the character from *Green Eggs and Ham*. Use the same "open to all possibilities strategy" as you learn more about yourself and your potential opportunities beyond high school. Let's get started reviewing the first key skill for success.

"You are today where your thoughts have brought you; you will be tomorrow where your thoughts take you."
~ James Allen

TIME

WHAT IS THE one element that most people feel they never have enough of? Time.

If you feel like you don't have enough time, you want to make a specific plan for how you use your time. Prioritize your schedule to spend the majority of your time on the most important things to you. Give yourselves the time to develop and execute a plan to move ahead based on your unique genius. Planning requires time for research and exploration; it's not all on an easily documented menu because what you do is unique to you only. Use your precious time wisely.

In this first Concept section, you will learn:

1. How to make time for your *Project of You Plan*

2. How to improve your time management skills

3. How you stay motivated to accomplish a goal

4. What an Accountability Partner is and why you need one

YOU CAN'T TURN BACK TIME

GIVE YOURSELF THE time to figure out your plan!

Your time at school, sports practice, play practice, karate lessons, SAT prep classes, and any other activities that you might do is planned for you on a set schedule. You do those activities based on someone else's schedule. Making your personal *Project of You Plan* will require you to budget your time to read this book, learn the key skills for success, and do the exercises included.

Time is the most important component of any great plan. Giving any idea the time needed for true exploration is the first key skill for success.

Think about choosing your path beyond high school? If you are a junior or senior, now is your time to do this exploration. If you are not a junior yet, it's never too early to begin planning for your decision. I've spoken to students who have begun this exploration process as early as seventh grade. You have to get to know yourself and what you want as well as finding time to research potential colleges, GAP year options, technical school programs, possible career paths, college majors, and any other possibilities for you.

Why put the time in now? You need to find the personal "best fit" options for your future based on your unique situation. Making your plan for life beyond high school offers many more choices and options than moving from one grade to the next during your K-12 years. It will require time for research, discovery and planning to create your plan.

Write this quote down, as a reminder to live for today, on a post-it note, index card, or make it your desktop screensaver:

Tomorrow is too late,

Yesterday is over,

Now is exactly the right moment so start.

I received a package from Seth Godin, an author and thought leader, and the front of the box had this quote on it. I keep the box in my office where I can see it to remind me that time is limited.

Keep that on your desk as a great reminder that time is precious and it can't be turned back.

If you don't feel like you even have an inkling of who you are and what you want to do even in a general sense, there is no better time than now to get to know yourself.

When should you start? Per my colleague, educational consulting expert Jamie Dickenson, you can begin as early as eighth grade walking college campuses, just to see what college is about.

You can begin visiting colleges, considering GAP year plans, exploring post high school career options, doing informational interviews, job shadowing, internships and thinking about what you want as soon as you are ready and make the time.

Many students don't start until junior or senior year and they make great plans. The key is to start; now is a great day to start your research.

Forward thinkers create a plan, focus on the plan, and execute the plan. Procrastinators, just talk about the plan, get distracted with minor things and postpone the plan. - We don't need time management, we need life management with purpose."
~ Farshad Asl

Consider the quote below, and remember to give yourself the time needed to be able to tell me or anyone who asks you: who you are, where you want to go, and how you plan to get there.

If you ever feel like I don't get you,
Please keep trying to explain,
I promise I will try with all my heart to understand,
If you can make me understand, then I know you know,
And there is nothing better.
~ Brenda Jo March

YOUR TIME IS NOW

DID YOU KNOW there are 168 hours in every week? How much time can you devote to your Project of You? Do you know how you spend your 168 hours of time in your week? Are you making the best use of your time? Remember the time spent on your *Project of You Plan* is an investment in YOUR future.

If you break out your 168 hours, you should be spending approximately 56 hours of that sleeping. I don't recommend that you take time away from sleep. Many studies have proven the importance of getting the right amount of sleep on your physical and mental health. Being at school for approximately seven hours per day is a total of 35 hours per week. That leaves approximately 77 hours per week for homework, eating, socializing, sports, family time, downtime, etc.

Out of that 77 remaining hours, I recommend that you dedicate a minimum of two hours per week to work on your plan. You will still have 75 hours left for your other activities. Obviously you can spend as much time as you want and the more time you spend, the more you will get out of it. The key is to dedicate time towards making your plan.

Total hours 168
School -35
Sleep -56
Free time 77
Project of You -2
You will still have a lot of Free time 75

Plan the two hours you will dedicate at the same time each week so that it becomes a consistent habit and a part of your calendar. Pick a time that will not have conflicts with your other activities. Making this plan is not a homework assignment; it's an investment in your future.

While this book is not focused on time management, it is important to budget your time to do a thorough *Project of You Plan*.

If you need to learn to better budget your time, here are a few ideas.

1. For 1 typical weekday and 1 typical weekend day, log your time. You can download the **My Time Worksheet** from my website: www.marchforwardconsulting.com or utilize the **My Time Worksheet** in your **The Project of You workbook.** This will allow you to see how you are spending your time and make choices.

2. Review the log with a trusted advisor or accountability partner

3. Make a list of your tasks

4. Prioritize your tasks

5. Learn to say NO if you are overbooked

6. Make a plan and be sure to include time for your Project of You reading and research

7. Learn to focus, turn off your cell phone, the TV and other distractions while you are reading or researching or doing other important work

8. Make a to do list each night and update it daily. This can be a simple word document or notes filed on your laptop or phone or it can be a paper based list, whichever works best for you

Developing effective time management skills will serve you well in any path you choose beyond high school. Perhaps you feel like you need help with time management skills.

And what are other students feeling? A random survey done by MarchForwardConsulting of high school students from 8 different local PA high schools, regarding their greatest fears around transitioning from high school to college and/or career, showed that the biggest concern is they feel is the need to improve their time management skills.

38% of students chose this as their top concern. Time management has become more difficult than ever in the past, given constant stimulation and interruption via technology.

Olivia Hunt, high school sophomore, additionally shared this feedback:

"Time management is a concern, because students have the freedom to choose exactly how hard the classes they take in high school are. You can challenge yourself with more difficult courses, or not. However with college every class is a vigorous one.

On top of that, college is setting you up directly for a career, so there's no 'choosing the easy classes' just to get by, but rather a pressure to excel in what you choose as your path. "

If you feel that you need additional time management training or tips, there are numerous programs and resources available on line as well as in-person trainings and many books on the subject. Again this is why you have to make strides to budget your time and be disciplined about it. Budgeting time to do the research necessary to make a plan for beyond high school is key to choosing the best option for you.

Would you consider the time to make the decision for a potential $200,000 investment a high priority? If you decide to go to college, the investment could be as much as $200,000 or more. If you decide to start your own business, it could be even more expensive. Given those numbers, I assume that you will consider this a priority.

Your plan is important and it's important to consider who you are and what you want rather than the potential status that might be associated with your beyond high school choice. In other words, there are many people who select colleges, majors, technical schools, gap years, or start careers that aren't right for them based solely on name brands, advertising, or on another's advice. They may have made those choices without exploring what they want and increasing their self-awareness. In many cases they have to transfer schools, change majors, find a new career, or any other significant change that costs them time and money. Imagine how much more meaningful any of those experiences could be if their path was clear and they could have streamlined their focus.

Budget your time for the most important project you have been assigned to date. Build time into your personal calendar for time alone to develop your plan. And also build in time for collaboration with others and research and exploration.

Decide now what time slots in your week will be for Project You. Pick at least two dedicated hours per week but don't limit yourself to two hours if you have more available time. The time and energy you put in now will save you money and time in getting to and through college or a gap year or a technical school or making money in your chosen career. Everything you do to prepare will streamline and focus the process for you.

Set a time that you can stick to and do not allow distractions to interrupt you.

You will read about your support options in the following chapters, perhaps finding one or more accountability partners or hiring a coach or educational consultant to work with you as a group. There are many options but don't make this crucial decision without the research, support, guidance, and time that it deserves.

Now is as good a time as any to begin this process. It's never to late or too early to begin developing a strong sense of self and most importantly, accepting and embracing the person you are and can become. You don't have to wait until junior or senior year to begin discovering what you want and how you are going to get there, and developing your plans beyond high school. Junior and senior year are two of your busiest years both academically and socially so be sure to budget the time needed to begin exploring and researching your options. Completing a time use assessment log will help you see how you are spending your time, and then you can prioritize which activities are most important to you and your future.

BE READY WHEN THE GUN GOES OFF

WHEN A RACE starts, sometimes a gunshot signals the start of the race. While marching forward beyond high school is not a race, it is important to make a plan and prepare. Pink Floyd did a song called "*Time*" and one of the verses talks about being ready when the gun goes off. I believe it's symbolic of being young and feeling like you are waiting for the starting gun to go off - meaning marching forward into the adult world. Starting your life as an adult requires preparation. In the song they refer to the concept "no one tells you when to run" so you could miss the hypothetical starting gun if you aren't prepared. All the academic preparation that you do as part of your typical school is important but you also need to have a plan for what happens next.

Who will make sure you are ready when the gun goes off, when you leave high school?

You will. By completing the process of the Project of You, you will be ready and know when to run; you won't miss the starting gun.

SETTING GOALS

To be ready you need to learn to set and reach your goals. It is important to be accountable to yourself and to have self-discipline. This means setting a goal and making it happen. Setting and accomplishing goals is a key skill for success in your future.

> *"Our goals can only be reached through a vehicle of a plan, in which we must fervently believe, and upon which we must vigorously act. There is no other route to success."*
>
> *~ Pablo Picasso*

No book about marching forward would be complete without a chapter on goal setting. Although you may be rolling your eyes saying, "yeah, yeah, it's good to have goals," this gives you an opportunity to really assess what you've declared you want in life. Are you satisfied with where you are at in your school career, future plans, health, personal relationships and extra-curricular activities? If not, it's time to write out your goals! Writing your goals down creates a true intention. What have you set as your benchmarks for success in each of those areas?

J.C. Penney was a man who didn't mince words. (He also appreciated a great deal.) Once he said, *"Give me a stock clerk with a goal and I'll give you a man who will make history. Give me a man with no goals and I'll give you a stock clerk."*

You want to set goals so you have purpose and direction in your actions. And, not to stress you out, if you don't have goals, you may find yourself waking up one night in a cold sweat after realizing you're not ready for the next phase of your life. Hello… I just graduated… what do I do next beyond high school?

Making up your mind and setting a goal - one that challenges you without breaking you - gives you something to aim for and something to work for. And when you do that, you never lose. This one step of selecting a goal and working to achieve it gives you purpose and intent. It gives you a life worth living.

Changing Direction?

The late, great Jim Rohn said, "***You cannot change your destination overnight, but you can change your direction overnight.***" Actually, with all respect to Mr. Rohn, it doesn't even take that long to change direction. It simply takes a split second to make a decision. The main thing is to make that decision to go from what you don't want, to what you do.

"Do not run from something, run to something"

A common goal-setting technique involves the acronym SMART-- perhaps you've heard of setting SMART goals.

Smart stands for:

Specific

Measurable

Attainable

Realistic

Timely

First, you want your goal to be specific. A specific goal sets you up for success and gives you the ability to accomplish it. It also means you'll recognize it when you achieve the goal. You need to think like a reporter when you're setting a specific goal - asking yourself who, what, where, when, why and, instead of how, which. (Meaning which requirements and constraints can you identify?)

Second, it should be measurable. What numbers can you assign to your goal to measure your progress and attainment? This will help you stay on track and give you reason to celebrate when you accomplish the goal.

Next, verify your goal is attainable. You want to not only identify the steps you'll take to achieve your goal, but the time frame involved. At the same time, realize you'll grow along the way, adopting an attitude of confidence and great capacity as you meet your mini-goals along the way.

Then comes "realistic," as you want your goal to represent an objective that's not only attainable, but also one you're willing to work towards. At the same time, don't make it easy but something that will represent progress and growth on a number of levels, say personally and professionally.

Finally, the last letter T can be for "timely." You don't want to meander towards your goal, but instead create a sense of urgency. Having a nebulous date sometime in the future will not cut it. Instead you want to anchor your goal within a specific timeframe. To make sure it is achievable, ask yourself what else needs to happen -both in and out of your control -to make the goal happen. If it's realistic and has happened before, it can happen again!

Just a note--the T in SMART can also stand for tangible. A goal is tangible when you can experience it with one of your five senses. Some say that you have a better chance of making it happen if you think tangible, because it will become more "real."

Download the **My Goals Worksheet** from my website: www.march-forwardconsulting.com or utilize the **My Goals Worksheet** in **The Project of You workbook.** Write at least two SMART goals for the next week.

Now comes the hard part once you have written down and acknowledged your goals - actually accomplishing them. This means that you need to be personally responsible. You need to be accountable to yourself. Some people have a stronger sense of self-discipline than others so be honest with yourself as you read through the next section on reaching goals. Don't feel any shame in asking for help to be held accountable; many people need that assistance.

"It's better to be at the bottom of the ladder you want to climb than at the top of the one you don't."

~ Stephen Kellogg

REACHING GOALS

THINK BACK TO any goals you have created in the past to decide whether or not you are a person who has natural self-discipline or who has developed that quality.

Do the exercise below to confirm whether or not you need to learn to be more accountable to yourself to reach your goals or perhaps you need to ask for assistance.

Download the **My Accomplished Goals Worksheet** from my website: www.marchforwardconsulting.com or utilize the **My Accomplished Goals Worksheet** in **The Project of You Workbook.**

Let's start with this exercise:

List a minimum of three goals that you have accomplished in column one.

In column two, list all the reasons why you feel you were successful; what were your motivators?

Some examples might be:

1. a parent or guardian held me accountable,
2. a teacher held me accountable,
3. I was part of a team and didn't want to let them down,
4. I knew it was required and didn't want to let myself down,
5. I pre-planned and budgeted my time and held myself accountable.

Review your list and if all the answers in column two are similar to examples one, two and three, try to think of an example of a goal you accomplished that would qualify for example four or five. In other words, think of a time that you held yourself accountable to reach your goal. This is what you will need to do to be ready for life beyond high school.

If you aren't able to list at least three goals that you can answer example four or five in column two, you will need to work on your personal accountability skills. If you need help with improving your personal accountability skills, ask a parent or guardian, teacher, coach, mentor, friend, or another trusted person to help you form new habits. You will need personal accountability skills to both complete your *Project of You Plan* and for success in your future beyond high school. Read on to learn about finding an accountability partner.

In other words, there is no time like now to get started. If you make a large investment in college or a technical school or some other training after high school but aren't happy with your options when you finish, you may feel like you missed the gun by investing your time and money in a path that doesn't work for you. The key is to find the starting line and be ready when the gun goes off.

You may notice that I am a true music fan. I often reference ideas from song lyrics. Music, movies and art are a reflection of life and we can learn much from them. Clearly these types of songs were written by people who felt these same struggles and feelings and they are expressing them in the hopes that you will learn something from them such as: *understanding that no one tells you when to run.*

Whether you are a sports fan and need to develop your game plan or a music fan that needs to write your own lyrics, the key is that you need to work on the five key skills for success because they are not learned **instinctively**. Learning to budget your time and develop and reach goals are not easy skills to master. In talking to many adults, these can be challenges at any point in life. Like any important skill, if you keep trying, "practicing" what you have learned, it will become easier.

> *"The greatest danger for most of us is not that our aim is too high and we miss it, but that it is too low and we reach it."*
>
> *~ Michelangelo*

FIND AN ACCOUNTABILITY PARTNER

WHAT IS AN accountability partner? Making an agreement with another person to help them keep a commitment or follow through on a goal is called an accountability partner. This term originated in the weight loss industry but is now used more broadly to help your partner reach most any type of goal or complete a personal or business project.

One way to better manage your time is to schedule regular meetings with another person to discuss your progress. While you may be willing to *let yourself down,* if you committed to do something with another person, you won't want to *let them down.* Learning to be personally accountable or finding accountability partners will be a key to success and help you as you develop your personal *Project of You Plan.* Many successful people use accountability partnerships to accomplish goals.

Having an accountability partner is priceless! Imagine someone who knows what you are trying to accomplish and checks in with you to make sure you are reaching your goals. Who couldn't use that?

For you, an accountability partner could be a teacher, a coach, a friend, a parent, a neighbor; anyone you respect that you feel truly wants the best for you. Choose someone who will be consistent and is able to have the difficult conversations to push you ahead if you are stuck and not reaching your goals.

Not having an accountability partner to help a person accomplish their goal is one reason 92% of people did not accomplish their New Year's resolution according to a University of Scranton study by Dan Diamond in Forbes.

Engage an accountability partner as you work through the five keys skills for success and develop your personal *Project of You Plan*.

Download the **My Accountability Partner Worksheet** from my website: www.marchforwardconsulting.com or utilize the **My Accountability Partner Worksheet** in **The Project of You Workbook.**

- List at least five people you would feel comfortable asking to be your accountability partner in the first column.

- Then list the reasons that you feel they would make a good accountability partner.

- Next, based on your list, prioritize your choices.

- Last, list the potential times that you have available to meet with your accountability partner for at least 30 minutes per week.

- Reach out to your potential accountability partners in the priority order listed to confirm that they are willing and available to make this commitment to you. Depending on who it is, you may be able to reciprocate and hold them accountable to their goals also.

- Agree to a weekly meeting; decide where it will occur, via phone or in person, at your home or your school or another location, or via Skype or face time

- Block this time out on your calendar for a minimum of three months to start

- At the end of three months time, mutually agree if this accountability partnership is working

- If it is working, book another three months

- If it is not working for you, be honest and fair and if needed, make the potentially difficult decision that you feel it's in your best interest to find a new accountability partner

- Go back to your original list and find a new partner and start the process over

- Or if you need to do so, make a new list of potential accountability partners based on what you have learned in the first three months

- And after the list is completed, repeat the process

An accountability partner is an important person in your *Project of You Plan* development. Many adults engage or hire accountability partners or coaches to accomplish personal and professional development goals. Don't take this lightly; successful people don't get there alone, they have coaches or accountability partners of some type.

Let me share an example of two high schools who became accountability partners and have added to their success.

Two students I met at one of my workshops several years ago, Megan and Kelly, were already friends and came together to the workshop. The workshop was focused on increasing self- awareness, discovering your path, and tips for success beyond high school. They both were honest about the fact that they didn't want to be there, but their parents had insisted that they come and see what they could learn. We did several role-plays and exercises around developing self-awareness and non – conformity, discovering who you are and not feeling like you need to follow the crowd.

During these discussions, Megan and Kelly shared that there was a girl in their school, Jenna, who was a complete non-conformist and did what made sense for her regardless of what others thought of her or said to her. Megan and Kelly thought perhaps it was time for them to adopt

Jenna's attitude and stop following the crowd at school. We discussed them developing an accountability partner relationship to hold each other accountable to make this change. I received emails from both of them separately later that evening sharing how glad they were that their parents made them come to the workshop.

Each of them also asked if I could work with them on their Project of You Plan development and help them establish an accountability partner relationship. I suggested that perhaps I could work together with both of them at the same time to decrease the expense to them and increase the strength of their accountability partner relationship. They were able to help each other not only become non-conformists but also to develop strong plans for themselves for beyond high school. They are both happy and successful in college now.

Even though they are attending different colleges, they still continue both their friendship and a weekly accountability partner session to review goals and progress. Megan and Kelly both feel this partnership has made a huge contribution to their current success and focus.

So decide if you want to establish an accountability partner relationship. Once you go beyond high school, it's up to you to find an accountability partner if you feel you need one. I think everyone should have an accountability partner, or coach or mentor at every point from high school through early career. Most largely successful people have coaches or mentors for their specific focus areas. There are numerous resources on line for learning more about these personal development key skills for success. In addition, many coaches offer free webinars online. Many coaches also offer group coaching sessions, which makes it more affordable.

Many people generally think of coaching in relation to careers in sports or music or acting - someone like Beyonce or Jordan Spieth or LeBron James. Clearly they all have coaches and it has helped them be successful.

The article below provides an interesting perspective on coaching.

Would a person think of a surgeon needing a coach? Here is an excerpt from an article by a surgeon who realized the benefits of hiring a coach to sharpen his surgery skills:

Personal Best

Top athletes and singers have coaches. Should you? BY ATUL GAWANDE

Elite performers, researchers say, must engage in "deliberate practice"—sustained, mindful efforts to develop the full range of abilities that success requires. You have to work at what you're not good at. In theory, people can do this themselves. But most people do not know where to start or how to proceed. Expertise, as the formula goes, requires going from unconscious incompetence to conscious incompetence to conscious competence and finally to unconscious competence. The coach provides the outside eyes and ears, and makes you aware of where you're falling short. This is tricky. Human beings resist exposure and critique; our brains are well defended. So coaches use a variety of approaches—showing what other, respected colleagues do, for instance, or reviewing videos of the subject's performance. The most common, however, is just conversation.

To read the full article, search for this link:
http://www.newyorker.com/magazine/2011/10/03/personal-best

There is not a person or profession in the world that couldn't benefit from working with an expert coach as an individual or in a group but it is not required to complete your *Project of You Plan.*

Unless your future work does not involve another human being, a very highly unlikely possibility, you will always have to be accountable to someone – your boss, your clients, your investors, or your employees.

As you think of the five key skills for success, some would call these skills the tools for the game of life? The world is now made up of so many games. Transitioning from childhood to adulthood is just another game where you have to learn the rules, characters, and skills needed to conquer.

It's all a game but you need to clearly recognize that you are the only person who can move your piece ahead to decide where you want to land. This is true during all points in your life but many people have parents, teachers, coaches, and other caring adults that will hold you accountable and help you move forward during your K-12 years. In many cases, once you transition beyond high school, you will have fewer people holding you accountable. You can ask for help from an educational consultant, coach, mentor or ask a friend to be an accountability partner and start your journey together.

Learn to be accountable to yourself and how to develop accountability partners because they are worth their weight in gold!

IS KARAOKE FUN?

HAVE YOU EVER done karaoke? Did you have fun? It can be fun if you can laugh at yourself. Have you ever done something without spending any time preparing and wished you had spent the time preparing? I'd like to share a personal story to illustrate a point about the importance of giving you time for preparation.

I believed my dream was to be either a singer or a drummer or both in a rock band; what could possibly be a better life? I thought I wanted to be on stage until I tried it.

On a cruise with friends, during karaoke, my friend Cindy and I decided to do a song. We ran through the list and "thought we both knew the lyrics and tune" to an old song by Cher, "If I could turn back time". We "stumbled" through it. But we didn't know the words or the tune, and I have many gifts but singing is not one of them It was bad. Sometimes karaoke performances are funny but I don't think we even accomplished that!

Being on stage knowing it's not going well may be one of the worst feelings in the world in my opinion. Clearly it keeps many people from even trying. Once we recovered from our sense of disappointment and embarrassment, we agreed to no more karaoke that cruise. And Cindy laughed and said to me.

"I wish I really could turn back time....to before we did that".

I can't hear that song without thinking about her saying that! So witty and also so true for how both of us felt at that point.

Another great reminder that most great performances, done well, require preparation and planning!

Have you ever done something without preparing and wished you had prepared?

I don't want you to feel that way about your Project of You Beyond High School Plan.

Give your *Project of You Plan* the time and preparation it deserves, not last minute karaoke!

TIME:

Before marching forward, have you:

1. Committed a set time for 2 hours per week to your *Project of You Plan*

2. Organized your materials in either an online file or bought a notebook or folder

3. Reviewed your time assessment log and made adjustments if necessary

4. Learned the skills for you to develop and attain goals

5. Committed to an accountability partner relationship

If yes, keep reading. If not, go back and complete these to do's.

Now that you have completed this TIME key skill section, do you feel like you have more clarity about how to manage your time? You are ready to move onto the Self Awareness Key skill section.

SELF AWARENESS

NOW THAT YOU have agreed to a time commitment, accountability partner, and organized your materials it's time to beginning improving your self-awareness.

My definition of being self-aware is:

understanding who you are both inside and outside by discovering your individual:

- **traits**: gifts, passions, and challenges
- **feelings**: core values, desires, what makes you happy, and fears
- **behaviors**: personal style, preferred communication & learning methods, and your curiosity.

You will be the person who needs to sell yourself to a college or trade school or employer beyond high school and to do that, you will need to be able to share your traits, feelings and behaviors.

Would you buy a product from someone who couldn't tell you all the details about the product? No.

Can you sell yourself? Considering and documenting your traits, feelings and behaviors will help you to sell yourself to a school or employer beyond high school.

In this concept section you will:

1. Learn whether you are a specialist or multipotentialite
2. Develop your Mantra
3. Determine what makes you happy
4. Recognize the importance of your curiosity
5. Learn to follow your heart, intuition, and conscience
6. Develop belief in your unique gifts

After completing the readings and exercises in this section, you will have stronger self-awareness that will make it easier to complete your *Project of You Plan* and march forward beyond high school.

ARE YOU A SPECIALIST OR
A MULTIPOTENTIALITE?

IN TERMS OF career choices, there are two kinds of people in this world - specialists and multipotentialites. You may know what a specialist is: a person who chooses one of their talents and limits their focus to one career path. But what is a multipotentialite? A multipotentialite is a person who has multiple talents that could become a great career for them. In many cases, multipotentialites have a difficult time settling on a career path for that reason. This is in comparison to a person who is a specialist; an example might be someone who is a gifted writer and loves writing so it's a clear path.

You don't need to decide at this moment which type of person you are, but it's important to be aware that both types are needed in this world. Either type is a positive trait, and the TED talk referenced below will help you better understand this. It's important not to feel pressured to become a specialist if that is not your true self. Embrace whichever path you choose and know that being either a multipotentialite or a specialist, you will find success if you decide on your path.

There are several TED talks on multipotentiality so if you want to better understand the term multipotentialite, watch this TED talk by searching for:

"Why some of us don't have one true calling", to find it.

Making your *Project of You Plan* may require more research if you are a multipotentialite. If you are a multipotentialite, I recommend narrowing your Beyond High School Plan down to two main areas of interest. Think of yourself like a rainbow - it has so many brilliant colors but the light is muted. You want to develop more of a laser focus to make the most of your plan for beyond high school. You can continue to explore your other areas of interest but narrow your choices after completing your research in the upcoming chapters.

A specialist whose interests lie mostly within a single field will be able to more easily develop their *Project of You Plan*.

Some people, the specialists, know what they are good at and what they want, often from a young age. The specialists' clarity and ease of their *Project of You Plan*s may seem extremely lucky to multipotentialites; they appear to be born knowing their dream.

Perhaps these specialists love to sing and can easily match pitch. Or they are a natural at a sport or gifted in math or some other academic pursuit. As soon as the adults in their world such as parents, coaches and teachers, discover their talent, they are encouraged and praised to the point that even if they wanted to do something else, they likely would not. This is not always a good thing because it can prevent them from exploring other options and getting to truly know if that is their passion. As long as you are true to yourself, you will be happy and successful.

Others are inspired at a young age and decide they want to become specialists such as a doctor, a teacher, an artist, or any other easily describable career. They make their connection and head down that path and do not stray. If they really know themselves and picked correctly, they stay focused through college and then enjoy their rewarding life's work.

Each person has their own unique genius, their own circumstances, and their own interesting unique life path that I refer to as their back-story. Each person follows a different route that is their own; there are no Google maps to chart your individual path.

During my career exploration work with a student named Kayla, she was frustrated that that she had so many potential choices. She wished her path could be as clear as it seemed to be for her friends that were specialists. Kayla had friends in high school with clear plans for a path and total connection to their personal plan. She wanted so much to be a specialist vs. a multipotentialite.. She so badly had wished to be one of them when she was younger. Why? It appeared so much easier than her "apparently scattered" plan.

She went to college planning to be a vet because she loved animals and enjoyed learning biology. But she also loved and could see herself in a career in art, fashion design, education, music, social work, or psychology. She was discouraged from many of her choices due to what the she was told about the income potential in some of her other areas of interest.

Without doing any true career exploration, just knowing that she loved animals, Kayla entered college majoring in veterinary medicine. During the summer after her freshman year of college, she found an internship working at veterinary clinic. Her second day there she assisted with two dogs who were injured with no chance of full recovery. The doctor had to talk with the owners and then assist them in saying their final good-byes to their pets. Kayla did not consider this portion of a career as a veterinarian. She asked the doctor how often she had to assist people in saying goodbye to their beloved pets. The doctor said she has to do this several times each week. that it is part of the job, and she has learned to accept it as helping to relieve their pet's suffering. Kayla gave this a lot of thought and believed that she would not want to have to help people say goodbye to their pets regularly. She decided at that point in time to research some other potential career paths.

Kayla did numerous informational interviews and job shadows during that summer, exploring several other interest areas. She spoke to a neighbor who was a freelance graphic designer. Kayla had always loved art especially painting, but she had been told it would be difficult support herself as an artist and it is just a hobby. Her neighbor allowed her to spend a half- day job shadowing her while she worked developing various types of designs for her clients. She saw that her neighbor did a variety of work from interactive web design to hard copy print ad designs. Kayla loved the creativity and variety of her neighbor's work. She went home and researched careers and salaries in graphic design as well as college programs in graphic design.

Kayla is almost done her graphic design degree program. She has done several internships and loved the work. She is excited about the opportunities and knows where to find work when she graduates. She also volunteers at the SPCA to work with animals. She is also open to eventually fulfilling some of her other potential choices: perhaps considering education, possibly teaching graphic design in the future or using her design skills in fashion design, also a strong interest.

My life experience is another example of multipotentiality. I went to college planning to major in psychology, without doing enough research and feeling a true connection and potential outcome to my plan. I made my plan based on one personal experience. I didn't have a true connection. I wasn't self-aware and I was interested in so many other things. But were those other ideas potential college majors or career paths, or were they potentially good choices for college electives and future hobbies? I also thought I could be a choreographer, or an occupational therapist, or a corporate CEO, or a drummer in a rock band, or the manager of a rock band. I picked psychology simply because I had to pick something and thought I could solve a problem. It turned out to be a good choice for me but when I first left high school, I wasn't really sure. I needed more exploration to reach the point of connection and truly committing to a plan. Looking back, I wish I had been given information about the five keys to success earlier in my life. Being more self-aware may have given greater clarity on my path.

I was so envious of the specialists and their clarity and connection that I wished they had a potion I could drink to find my specialty. But now that I understand it, I embrace my multipotentiality with every fiber of my being. My hope for you is that you discover whether you are a specialist or a multipotentialite and embrace your future possibilities in either case.

I truly consider myself a multipotentialite. If I were to list all of my post college professional titles, it might surprise you. I had lots of great, fulfilling, interesting experiences in various industries. Each one was a wonderful learning experience and helped me to become who I am now.

I enjoyed most of my positions for different reasons and learned in every case. I didn't stay very long at the ones I didn't enjoy, and they helped me rule out what I didn't want. This is also important learning. Don't worry - whatever you choose will help you find the right path as long as you know who you are, what you want. and you work hard to make it happen.

Many young adults have not identified a career choice that speaks to them either because they haven't become clear in the five key skills to success, or because they haven't researched and learned enough about the potential options that make sense for them, or both these ideas. In other cases, a student has been successful in most endeavors they have tried and a specific interest area hasn't risen to the top of their list. I believe that we need to teach everyone to become comfortable with the five key skills to success through personal research, self-awareness training, and career exploration focused work. I love the term "Learn to be still". This is also the title to a great song by the Eagles. The song asks, "Where do I fit in?" Only you can decide where you fit in but learning to be still and thinking about who you really are will help you decide where you fit in.

How many times in your life have you done something because you felt like you had to or you should or it is what someone else would want you to do? Now it's about you and following your internal guides. Do you need to find out "Where do I fit in?"

Throughout the exercises and readings you will discover what you need to know about yourself. You will also learn how you fit into the world beyond high school. Regardless of whether you discover that you are a specialist or multipotentialite, both are needed so don't worry. The key is knowing yourself and being able to share who you are with a potential college, technical school, and gap year or career interviewer. All types of industries need both specialists and multi-potentialites in their businesses and organizations because both contribute differing strengths and skills to their workplace community.

YOUR MANTRA

A MANTRA IS a motivating chant that you repeat over and over to yourself to inspire you. An example might be a person running a marathon who says "I can do this!" or "I'm ready for the next mile!" The word Mantra comes from a Sanskrit word meaning "a sacred message or text, or charm, or counsel." Mantras are often repeated silently in your mind during meditation. You can create your own mantra to help you better define what you want and also motivate you to achieve your personal goals.

My belief is that by reading this material and giving yourself the time and energy needed, you will find your mantra for what I believe is all anyone needs to be in life:

HHSS: happy, healthy and self - supporting.

If you have another acronym that describes what you want for your life, feel free to write it down and use it as your mantra. If you have a phrase that you already use as your mantra - that's great. If you don't have a mantra yet, try to come up with at least three words that could become your mantra and help motivate you as you continue making your plan. The key is that you know what you want so you can make it happen.

Let me give you an example. Perhaps being extremely wealthy is your first priority and you also want to be famous and extremely fit. In that case, your mantra might be:

WFF – wealthy, famous & fit.

If that's you - know it and own it!

Here's another example from a colleague, Diane:

She called it her personal 4H's: **Healthy, Helpful, Harmonious, And Hilarious**

She wanted to find a career that allowed her to be healthy and be around healthy people. She wanted to help people, wanted to be in harmony with nature, and wanted to use her well-developed sense of humor to make people laugh.

Diane decided that she could achieve that by becoming a personal trainer, specializing in outdoor workouts and incorporating humor into her training. Weather permitting, she scheduled her sessions at outdoor locations, such as parks, or bike trails or golf courses or other locations near her office or her clients' homes. This reinforced a connection with nature for her clients as well as incorporating fitness training. Diane also believed that being connected to nature both motivated and relieved stress for her clients. She developed weekly emails with jokes related to fitness to send her clients. She also began each training session with a joke to get her clients to laugh and start in a happy place. Clients loved spending time with her and felt they were reaching their fitness goals while also connecting to nature and raising their spirits.

Now it's time for you to create your own personal mantra. If you are having trouble creating a mantra for yourself, talk to your accountability partner or a trusted friend and see if they can help you focus on the true you. Get together with a partner and brainstorm ideas for your mantra.

I usually suggest each of you getting a piece of paper and setting a timer for 10 minutes. During that time, write down all the words that you feel describe you or are important to you as a person. Then set the timer for another five minutes and circle the top ten words that you feel most strongly about. Then exchange lists with your partner and discuss why each one is important to you and prioritize your list. Once you can narrow your list down to the five or less words or ideas, decide if that is what you want to be your mantra for your *Project of You Plan.*

Keep your mantra in your online journal or folder or notebook but also write it on a post it note, index card or poster, and hang it somewhere you will see it daily to remind yourself what you want and who you are now. You can also add your mantra to your vision board if you have one. I don't cover vision boards but search vision boards if you are interested. Many people find vision boards very powerful.

WHAT MAKES YOU HAPPY?

MY DEFINITION OF happiness is having the mental and emotional feeling that your life is good - a feeling of well-being that can range from contentment to intense joy.

Imagine someone you know who doesn't often appear to be happy - perhaps an adult who constantly complains about their job or a friend who is always complaining and creating "drama".

Are these people that you enjoy spending your precious time with? No.

Do you think these people know what makes them happy? If they did, wouldn't they be making themselves happy? Perhaps not everyone knows what makes him or her happy. Now is a great time to recognize what makes you happy.

Being in a mental or emotional state of well -being comes from within you and is within your control. Knowing who you are and what makes you happy are extremely important and not necessarily intuitive. Many people go through their lives working to please others such as parents, friends, teachers, and coaches and never discovering what makes them happy. Your goal as part of your self-awareness concept exploration is to understand what makes you happy. It sounds simple but recognizing what makes you happy and writing it down and living it is not easy for many people.

Of course you can't be happy all the time; sad things do happen in the world. But many motivational speakers will tell you that if you never experience suffering, you will never recognize how wonderful happiness feels.

In a 2007 survey of more than 10,000 people from 48 countries published in Perspectives on Psychological Sciences, happiness was viewed as more important than success, intelligence, knowledge, maturity, wisdom, relationships, wealth and meaning in life.

I work with adults in many cases who feel they have never discovered what truly makes them happy. Learn what makes you happy now and you can take that feeling with you throughout your life.

Now I want you to do an exercise that requires at least 20 uninterrupted moments. Turn off your cell phone and your email and any other distractions. I will say that you can put on Happy by Pharell for inspiration, while you are giving this gift to yourself.

What makes you HAPPY?

Can you clap along? Do you know what Happiness means to you?

Inspire yourself with Happy by Pharell

Tune into your true feelings and make a list of what makes you happy. Sometimes defining what doesn't make you happy also helps you find clarity as you are deciding who you are and what you want.

To give you an example, I have done a quick five-minute list. Download the **My HHSS Worksheet** from my website: www. marchforwardconsulting.com or utilize the **My HHSS Worksheet** in **The Project of You Workbook.**

Taking the time to consider what YOU want and not what others suggest or tell you that you should do is an important part of beginning the journey to becoming my mantra for you: **HHSS – happy, healthy & self-supporting.**

Things that make me happy	Things I truly dislike
Music!!!!	Advanced Math!!!
Dancing	Writing technical documentation
Helping others find solutions	Following complicated directions
Reading	Running
Learning about the human brain	Memorizing facts
Understanding emotional intelligence	Editing/QA
Teaching others personal development	Balancing a checkbook
Coaching others	Accounting
Being coached by others	Complicated recipes
Organizing	Handling many minute details?
Planning	
Debating	
Writing non technical	
Dogs	
Flowers	
Being outside and connecting to nature	
Walking	

As you complete your "My HHSS Worksheet", don't just think about what makes you happy in relation to your future plan. All aspects of you are important, and each is a vital part of how you find your positive energy and how you fit into the world. I'm sharing a story about how one young woman discovered that music makes her happy and what that means to her. But I do want to give you a sense of how the energy, connection, and gift of music can enhance your life. I believe that finding a passion to fuel you even as times get tough is key to success.

You will read in Claire's life that music is her passion and has always been a part of her life peripherally. But Claire has never attempted to make a living in relation to music even though it makes her happy. Some things just make you happy and can always be a part of your world but they may become hobbies or activities that you continue to enjoy but not how you support yourself.

As a child, Claire believed that she had to be a performer. The first opportunity offered to her was the flute. Apparently the infamous "they" (the music education experts) had decided that a typical third grade student was ready to learn an instrument. And my guess is that many third graders are ready, but not all. Claire begged for a flute insisting she would practice. Perhaps some of you had the same experience?

Claire didn't know how to read music so that was her first challenge. Perhaps if it had been color coded like the game "Rock Band", it might have been easier for her but focusing on "those dots and lines in those small lines" was difficult. Then Claire had to learn to control her breath properly to control the air going into the flute. She had asthma and allergies so at times controlling her breath could be a challenge.

And last but not least, she had to learn where to put each of her fingers on the instrument to match the placement of the notes. Claire had to decide what the note on the page translated to and then move her fingers correctly, without a lot of time in between. She had to think about each of these things – the notes, the breathing, the fingers, and keeping time with her foot - all at the same time. For many of you fortunate people, this may have been an easy learning curve but not for Claire. Did I mention that Claire was borderline ADD and believed that it was worse when she was a child? She was not diagnosed or medicated as a child.

At first Claire went to lessons and tried to practice. The lessons were painful; the teacher and Claire and the other students in her lesson were all frustrated. Eventually she stopped practicing and the lessons became even more painful. Then she stopped going to the lessons. Claire would carry her flute with her to school because she couldn't bear to tell her mother that she had quit. When Claire told the teacher she was quitting, her teacher didn't even ask just once if she wanted to give it one more try. No surprise there but perhaps with patience and encouragement, Claire may have overcome the frustrations and difficulties or perhaps she should have been encouraged to try another instrument.

Claire really wanted to be a musician because she truly loved music and it made her feel happy! But at that moment in time, she decided that she wasn't good at music.

As an adult, she finally understood that the frustrations of her childhood don't need to be part of her world anymore, and that music can be an important part of life even if she doesn't make a living via music. Just to be happy, she is taking drum lessons now.

She told me she loves "Banging on the drum all day!"; when time and privacy allow it; drum practice is loud. Her story reminds me of Todd Rundgren's song, "Bang on the Drum All Day" – it's a rock classic! The main line from the song is "I don't want to work, I just want to bang on the drum all day" but that is not Claire's story. She has found a career in advertising that makes her happy and she enjoys learning the drums for fun because music makes her happy. She might sing, "I do want to work but I also enjoy banging on the drum!"

> *"Do we even know what it takes to be a happy, motivated, creative human being?*
>
> *I'm having trouble not worrying about my own children and I write books about this stuff "*
>
> *~ Kenneth Ginsburg MD University of Pennsylvania*

Develop your definition of what makes you happy to reference as you are learning about the potential career paths you can take beyond high school. Remember if you discover a new skill or concept that makes you happy add it to your list.

As an example, if you sign up to be a peer counselor in junior year and you realize that you enjoy counseling people, add that to your list.

Or if you take a part time job in a restaurant as a bakery assistant and you find that you love baking, add that to you list.

As you add these items to your list, consider what portion of the activity makes you happy. One example is Mark, a young professional who worked in an insurance agency and was not happy so he became a coaching client.

I asked Mark when he had been happiest in a job, and he stated when he worked as a manager in a restaurant in high school and college. In trying to discover what it was about it that made him happy, he realized that:

1. he liked the movement; he didn't like sitting at a desk all day,

2. he liked the creativity of developing a menu and cooking different meals,

3. he liked the problem solving when things didn't go as planned - someone called out sick, a customer sent back a dish, or they ran out of an item and had to substitute, etc

4. he liked the interaction with different people on a regular basis - staff and customers and vendors

So it wasn't simply about working as a restaurant manager. Mark now knew that any position he would potentially seek should have these qualities: movement, creativity, problem solving, and interaction with varied people. It didn't necessarily mean that he was destined to be in the restaurant business.

You can reference your list at any point in time and maintain it for life. No matter how old you get, having this in writing to remind you what makes you happy can help anytime you begin to lose focus. Knowing what makes you happy is not automatic.. You learn by trying new things just as you learned what you like to eat.

Trying new things and ruling out possibilities can be as important in career options. You can't decide something doesn't make you happy without trying it so be open to all possibilities and keep your list updated for reference.

THERE'S NO STOPPING YOUR CURIOSITY ABOUT?

CURIOSITY IS DEFINED as a quality related to inquisitive thinking such as exploration, investigation, and learning. The word "curiosity" denotes the behavior of being curious - the desire to gain knowledge or greater understanding of a new concept. Curiosity has sparked advancements in areas such as: human development, science, language, and industry.

Human beings and all living beings are naturally curious. Think about a dog and how they have to smell someone that walks into a room. Dogs are curious about who you are and what you smell like. This is one of the ways that dogs learn about their world. Our sense of smell also piques our curiosity; you know that amazing smell when you walk into a bakery with that freshly baked bread smell. Or think of a time when you walked into a kitchen or restaurant and smelled something amazing and wanted to know what it was and also wanted to try it. Your senses and your mind spark your curiosity.

Your natural curiosity began as a child and helped you to learn about your outside world. Trying new foods, touching objects, exploring nature and your home taught you what you needed to know. If you were curious about how the stove worked and turned it on and then touched it, your natural curiosity may have been stronger than an adult's warning that it was hot. But your curiosity taught you it was hot and shouldn't be touched - an important lesson but one best learned by listening to an adult. In many cases, that isn't how you learned but as long as you learned it the first time, that's fine.

Now as a young adult, you may be curious about many other things that are not as easy to discover. Perhaps you want to better understand the functioning of the human brain, or why some people have allergies, or how to program drones, or how Amazon can get your purchases to you so fast? What you are curious about will give you insights into your true self. There are numerous questions to ponder in this big crazy world but there are specific questions that interest you the most.

Your curiosity is what fuels your learning and one key to success for many is being a lifelong learner. Many people feel life is much more interesting and fulfilling that way. So pick something to focus on that maintains your curiosity.

Stay curious throughout this process about who you are. But be curious about everything that matters to you, dig a little deeper, do some research, and learn more. Obviously, many people currently have careers in fields that didn't even exist when I was in high school or college. Things change everyday at an amazingly rapid speed.

Advances in technology, medicine, e-commerce, and numerous other fields change the employment landscape regularly.

Now, more than ever, with all the technology and readily available information, you can find yourself traveling down numerous wormholes regularly.

You may find yourself reading a book or watching a documentary or movie, or doing research or simply being curious on your laptop, phone, or TV based on a conversation or comment that sparked your curiosity.

Perhaps you love technology, or medicine, or finance, or music, or art, or fashion and may not have considered the possible options in those areas as a potential future career path. Perhaps you have many interests and are trying to narrow your focus.

The most important question that I ask my clients to try and discover their natural curiosity is: What are you doing when you lose all track of time?

Download the **My Curiosity Worksheet** from my website: www.marchforwardconsulting.com or utilize the **My Curiosity Worksheet** in the Project of You Workbook.

Take the time to answer these questions thoughtfully and consider if you can find a common thread among them? Are all your answers related to a specific person or industry or passion? Look through your answers and begin to catalogue the topics encompassed. List the top three categories you feel are most represented such as: Sports, Technology, and Music or perhaps Fashion, Food and Fitness or Forensics, Robotics, and Politics. List these top three as headings and then fill in your answers underneath to determine which category you feel strongest about as far as your curiosity. Perhaps all three have equal value in your mind; no worries as you have two hours a week assigned to this project and you can research more than one path.

> *It is a miracle that curiosity survives formal education.*
>
> *~ Albert Einstein*

Whatever you choose to do beyond high school, it will be more enjoyable if you do something that connects to your natural curiosity. You may often hear this popular life advice - follow your passion - but many feel it should be replaced by the word curiosity. And I do agree with the "follow your passion" advice but it's easier said than done because to follow your passion, you need to find it. Finding your passion is not a learned skill or one that can be taught. Most people need help and it has been compared to trying to bake a cake without a recipe.

Here are some insights from people who believe their success is a direct result of their constant curiosity:

Eat, Pray, Love author **Elizabeth Gilbert** shared: **"Passion is rare; passion is a one-night-stand. Passion is hot, it burns. Every day, you can't access that…but every single day in my life there's something that I'm curious about—follow it, it's a clue, and it might lead you to your passion."**

Albert Einstein: "I have no special talent. I am only passionately curious."

Steve Jobs, in his Stanford commencement speech: **"Much of what I stumbled into by following my curiosity and intuition turned out to be priceless later on."**

Your curiosity is the tool that will help you find your passion; it creates the connection.

Albert Einstein: The important thing is not to stop questioning… Never lose a holy curiosity.

An example of staying connected to your curiosity is Nate's story.

One of my clients, Nate, is a great example of staying curious even if it means going outside of your comfort zone. Nate was bright, good at almost everything, and excelled academically but apparently not enough to get a scholarship.

I met Nate after he had left college, having completed his sophomore year successfully but not happily. Nate majored in accounting because everyone told him he should and it would be a financially lucrative field. Nate learned after two years of general education credits and some accounting classes that he did not like accounting and couldn't see himself doing accounting. Nate was not curious about any aspect of accounting.

What was Nate doing when he lost all track of time?

He had always been a big computer gamer and was curious about computer gaming. He loved it but couldn't see it as a career. He also didn't feel that he fit in socially at the college that he attended; apparently he hadn't readily found his tribe there.

So he decided to quit school and moved back in with his parents. They weren't happy and he wasn't happy - no surprise. When he came to meet with me, he was working at a restaurant as a busboy, again not happy but he had student loans to pay.

Nate struggled to make a plan of what he thought he wanted to do next. He couldn't see past his frustrations and sense of failure and confusion at that point. His parents' sense of disappointment was always there and it weighed him down also.

But he did believe he had done the right thing following his intuition to leave school at that point. This was key: no regrets. However, he did receive lots of tough reactions from well meaning family and friends who didn't agree with him not finishing college.

He needed help making a new plan as even most adults do when it comes to major life changes. Nate did a Curiosity assessment and the biggest theme was computer gaming. He shared his private dream with me. His "dream" was to write computer games but many adults he trusted had told him that computer game development is not a solid career plan. It's not a traditional career path from his parents' generation but the world is changing at warp speed. Nate agreed to research the possibilities rather than believing everything he had heard to date about how his best career path should be accounting.

He began exploring possibilities and trying to learn more about the back end of computer gaming - not just playing the games but understanding what went into them. He agreed to connect with several people in that field and set up informational interviews. As he is very shy, during one of his sessions, we collaboratively created a script that he could use to both set-up the meeting as well as what he wanted to learn during the meeting so he wasn't going in cold.

The research was easy for him because it stirred his natural curiosity.

He began to seem more energized and connected. He also agreed to add exercise back into his regular routine; feeling a somewhat situational depression, he had let that slip.

Nate learned a lot at through his research. One of the people he spoke to actually ran a software development firm. They didn't write computer games but it was a local company that was doing well and growing. He was invited to lunch to learn more and clearly the Director could see this young man's passion and potential so he offered him a full time job.

Nate couldn't believe it and didn't think he was ready, but he was curious to learn more and decided it was the right move for him. He was more than happy to say goodbye to restaurant work, which had no interest for him. This would give him more money to pay back his loans sooner and benefits also.

He loved the job, the people, the work, the culture; it was a perfect fit for him!

But we also agreed that finishing school was important so we continued working together to stay accountable to that goal.

Connecting to his natural curiosity even though it wasn't what others had recommended had turned out to be the best decision for him.

We worked together to develop a strategy for him finishing school in just 2.5 years based on utilizing online classes, summer classes, and testing out some general education credits. Nate asked me to continue working with him to hold him accountable.

It was a pleasure working with and watching him succeed and be energized by staying connected to his curiosity!

I hear this from many of my clients, as they begin to better understand who they are, what they want, and how to get there. They wish they had started earlier getting to know themselves and creating the life they want.

They wish they could "turn back time" but that is not possible. I remind them that NOW is the perfect time to start and better than not starting. The majority of my clients believe that we need to increase opportunities for self-exploration and real world experience at an earlier age. This is why I feel compelled to share this information with you.

Stay curious; it keeps you young and interested! Remember that it's up to you to find the answers you need to find. No one is going to come calling to make you:

the superhero of your own game of life or the rock star of your own band.

But if you want to make it happen, you can!

FOLLOW YOUR HEART,
INTUITION & CONSCIENCE

THERE ARE THREE internal guides that will help you make decisions: your heart, your intuition and your conscience. You may have already been using them to make your choices without even realizing it. They are strong and dependable guides if you are able to connect to them. I've defined them below and I'll give you some examples to consider. These are difficult key skills for success and it may take some practice to connect to these inner voices. I will refer to them as your inner GPS.

What does it mean to follow your heart?

This is not a reference to your physical heart, although many people feel the energy near the area of the heart. If any of you have an interest in alternative medicine, your heart is also known as the fourth chakra, the heart chakra. It is often associated with love, wisdom, and compassion. Following your heart is like listening to your inner GPS. You all have these inner voices within you to guide you but you have to be willing to listen.

What is intuition?

Intuition is challenging to define; despite the huge role it plays in our everyday lives. Steve Jobs called it, for instance, "more powerful than intellect." But however we put it into words, we all, well, *intuitively* know just what it is.

Pretty much everyone has experienced a gut feeling — that unconscious reasoning that propels us to do something without telling us why or how. But the nature of intuition has long eluded us and has inspired centuries' worth of research and inquiry in the fields of philosophy and psychology.

"I define intuition as the subtle knowing without ever having any idea why you know it," Sophy Burnham, bestselling author of *The Art of Intuition*, tells The Huffington Post. "It's different from thinking, it's different from logic or analysis ... It's a knowing without knowing." This definition is from a great article. If you want to learn more, search:

10 Things Highly Intuitive People Do Differently

By Carolyn Gregoire, Senior Writer, The Huffington Post

How can you follow your conscience?

A conscience is the voice in your head and the feeling in your heart, that tells you if something is right or wrong. Have you ever done something you knew wasn't ok, and then you felt uncomfortable in your heart or kind of yucky in your body? That's your conscience! If you've ever thought about doing something you knew wasn't ok, and a voice in your head said, "Maybe you shouldn't do that. You might get in trouble." That's your conscience! "Listen to your conscience" means you hear and feel the messages your conscience sends you and then you make a good choice.

You can't see it or touch it, but you can feel it in your mind and in your body. Your conscience knows all the rules you've learned about right and wrong. It knows what you've been taught about core values like honesty, responsibility, and respect.

Your conscience is like a super fast computer app that compares what you are about to do against your core values to help you know if your actions are right or wrong.

It's kind of like you put what you want to say or do into the "Conscience 3000-s Analyzer", and your conscience compares what you want against what you know is right and wrong. Then, it tells you the answer in your heart and in your mind.

This definition is from:

http://talkingtreebooks.com/definition/what-is-conscience.html

We all have our ways of making decisions and it's personal. After you do all the concrete thinking and researching and analyzing, how do you truly make a decision?

How do you decide what you really want?

People will often tell you to follow your gut, follow your heart, follow your intuition or if you remember Jiminy Cricket from Pinocchio, he had a song, *"Always let your conscience be your guide"*.

There are the negative inner voices that stop you from doing things by telling you that you aren't capable or by creating fear but your internal feelings - your heart, your intuition, your conscience - can help you determine what will work for you.

People will tell you to listen to your heart.

People will tell you to develop your intuition.

And let your conscience be your guide.

All three are great advice so be sure to recognize the little voices that you have inside you. Ignoring them to please someone else is never a good thing.

There are certain things that will be required of you such as attending 12 years of mandatory education but what you make of those 12 years is up to you.

What you do inside and outside of school is up to you. There may be many things you feel that you should do either because they have been offered to you, recommended to you or because they will look good on your transcript but that does not mean they are required.

Find the pursuits that align with you, that feel right to you intuitively. Do your best and work hard in the activities that are required. Recognize that you will have even more choices as you get older. That is why it is extremely important to learn to listen to your heart, recognize your intuition and follow your conscience.

Stop in the moment when you are being guided by these inner guides and consider how it feels.

Are you being guided by one of them or simply making an impulsive decision?

Even as a child you may have made tough decisions that the adults in your world may not have liked or thought were impulsive. Now perhaps you feel those tough decisions were you following your conscience, listening to your heart and using your intuition.

As a child, you wanted to please the adults in your world; this is natural. In many cases, you do what you are told regardless of whether or not you feel it is right for you. As a young child, you haven't learned enough about who you are and what you want to question. As you grow older, you begin to realize you can have a say in the decisions about how you spend your time and what you choose to do in and out of school.

Let me share an example about a young girl I knew who struggled with a decision in fifth grade.

Jane was gifted at playing the viola. She stuck with it for two years and then decided she had enough. She mentioned on many occasions that she no longer enjoyed it. But between the teacher and her family, she was always encouraged to continue because "she was so very good at it".

One day she reached her limit and without consulting anyone or looking back, handed her viola back to her teacher and said good-bye to her. The teacher suggested to her this was an indicator that she would consistently be a quitter but this was not the case.

The teacher called her family and explained how terrible this was down to using the three greatest magic words of encouragement for any parents, "Potential College SCHOLARSHIP"

Of course her family wanted to fix this and have her continue. Her family tried and tried to convince her to reconsider her decision. They even talked about forcing her to continue, using punishment for not going back to viola lessons. But with complete confidence, Jane shared that her other interests were stronger and in her long-term vision, there was not a viola. Without recognizing it, she followed her heart, her intuition, and her conscience. Her inner GPS told her that this was not a mistake for her. She had given it a lot of thought and knew this was right for her. She had already said goodbye to her instrument and her teacher.

Her teacher's negative comments about being a quitter rather than an encouraging and empathetic reaction to her decision had solidified her choice. Perhaps you have experienced a similar feeling of negative energy in the past. Jane's family realized that she tried and gave it her best and were proud of her ability to make that difficult decision. Jane told her family she would get a college scholarship for something else and she did! Jane could see that in her future vision and she did it!

Would her college application have been more appealing if she had played viola for eight years in an orchestra, but hated playing the viola. Imagine if she only played to potentially get a scholarship and please her parents. Jane might have missed out on opportunities for other great and amazing accomplishments that she did have on her application? And what doors might she not have opened if she had chosen to please others rather than herself and done what she had to do, should do, was supposed to do? Jane made space for new opportunities in her life. What her intuition and heart and conscience were telling her was the right answer for her. And she was able to listen to her inner GPS and make a difficult decision.

Have you had some tough decisions to make that weren't what your parents and guardians or coaches or friends wanted you to choose?

Learning to make the tough, go against the grain decisions is not easy but you can do it. If you have taken the time to listen to your inner GPS, you will be able to explain with complete clarity why you are making a tough choice. If you believe it is the right path for you and you feel it in your heart, and your intuition and your conscience are telling you that it is the right choice for you, then you have to listen to those voices. Ignoring your inner voices can cause you to feel stressed, lose your confidence, head down the wrong path, lose sleep, and become disillusioned with your life.

If you have truly researched the path you want to take and deliver the message of what you want to do and why you want to do it with complete confidence, there is no question in your mind. As you describe it to others with the same complete confidence, they will also have no doubt that it is the right decision for you. In talking with Jane about her decision, she described a silent voice within her telling her to "move on" at that moment. She had been thinking about it for a long time and didn't want to waste anymore of her precious time. It wasn't an impulsive decision but rather an inevitable choice. Her inner guides were so loud and clear that she had to follow them. And best of all, she described the feeling of leaving after returning her viola - sheer joy and relief at finally having made a decision. Jane was so emphatic in her decision that her family had to understand.

This is the feeling I want you to have as you move through life - the ability to follow your inner guides: your heart, your intuition, and your conscience. It may require practice and there are many tools online to practice meditation and other practices to connect to your inner GPS. I highly recommend meditation for cultivating your inner GPS.

Download the **My Listening to your Inner guides Worksheet** from my website: www.marchforwardconsulting.com or utilize the **My Listening to your Inner guides Worksheet** in **the Project of You Workbook.**

As an adult, you have to listen to your inner GPS and do what works for you regardless of what others tell you. Listen to their wisdom; in many cases it's helpful but if you have truly researched an option that makes sense for you and you can justify it, GO FOR IT!

As you move on past school into the working world where there are so many more choices, listening to your inner GPS from your heart, your intuition, and or your conscience will be even more important.

Students who have found their passion and focus are able to not only concentrate on them but also enjoy the time spent. With all this talk about lack of engagement in our corporate environment, how can we be surprised? Many simply choose a hobby or major or career because they are good at it. This isn't always the best reason, it is also not a good basis for choosing a path in life. If you don't enjoy it, it doesn't matter that you are good at it. Should you like a boy or girl because they like you? Or does the feeling need to be mutual? Forming a relationship just because someone likes you is not a good basis for a relationship unless the feeling is mutual.

We all need to find what we enjoy and are passionate about and stay focused.

Of course, there will be things that you have to do and you should do in your life. Every moment won't be fully focused on your future vision but if you never find your future vision, where is your center? What do you move towards when you don't know what path to take? This is when you need to learn to follow your heart, your intuition and your conscience. Below is an example of a student who learned this early in his college career.

Ryan was a good student who was very comfortable and socially active in high school. He didn't put a lot of time into deciding on his beyond high school path. He was a young man who generally believed in living in the moment. College was a far away idea. Ryan did end up choosing two schools to apply to and was accepted to both. They were both very different but he ended up choosing the larger school that was closer to his home. He also knew more students that already attended or were planning to go to that school. He chose a major that he thought sounded interesting but he hadn't done any true research about career options with that major.

Ryan did ok his first year but not the standard that he wanted to reach. When he told his parents that he didn't want to go back to school, they were shocked and disappointed but Ryan knew what he wanted and needed to do. Ryan explained to his parents that he felt he was wasting his and their money and it wasn't a good fit at that moment in time. He realized that he didn't have the self-discipline and personal accountability to do his best.

His parents were concerned that he was quitting college but Ryan wanted to finish school. He had given this a lot of thought and tapped into his heart, intuition and conscience and made a plan for himself. He shared his plan with confidence, planning to move home and go to the local community college and work part time. Ryan wanted both the structure of living at home and the option to gain more work experience while considering his career choices. Ryan knew his parents would be disappointed but he also followed his heart, intuition and conscience and felt confident this was the best choice for him at that moment. He had a successful year living at home and going to community college. He saved some costs on college living expenses and was able to make some extra money working part time.

During that year he explored several options for potential college majors, career paths, and looked at several different university programs to attend after completing his associate degree at community college. He chose a school that he didn't even consider as a high school senior. He attended three different colleges and graduated from college in four and a half years. This was a big accomplishment as many students take over four years without transfers. The year Ryan spent at home also decreased *his projected college debt amount as he didn't have to pay living expenses, and the community college was significantly less expensive than his original college choice. After much exploration and experiential learning, Ryan now has a career in business that he feels is the perfect fit for him.*

It was a tough decision for Ryan, knowing his parents and others felt that he would have better opportunities staying in his first college. In addition, some students and adults are more concerned with brand names and look down on community colleges. But clearly this was the right choice for Ryan, and he had the clarity to make the best decision for him by following his inner voices.

If you have tough choices to make, you need to practice learning to follow your inner GPS: your heart, your intuition, and your conscience won't steer you wrong. No one else can tell you what's best for you because you are the person that has to follow through with the *Project of You Plan* that you create, not anyone else. The term they use in the business world is "buy-in"; be sure to get your own "buy-in" before making a huge decision about your Beyond High School Plans.

YOU ARE WHAT YOU POST

WHAT DO YOU post on social media? Photos you would want college admissions officers and future employers to see? Comments that a potential mentor would be impressed by? Are you being a positive influencer? What you post on social media never goes away; it is always accessible, not erasable. Every post you add to any social media sites that you use is creating "your brand". Does what you post reflect the brand you would choose for your future?

Always be aware, anything that you type or post is accessible in the future. It is permanent in some format, online, in your cell phone records, in another person's cell phone records, in an email or on your laptop or tablet. Technology experts can trace anything you type or record back to you, so don't document anything you wouldn't be comfortable with someone else reading in the future.*

In speaking to many college recruiters and human resource professionals, after they review your resume, they do a search to learn more about you and who you are.

What results come up on the search when you enter your name? It is important to know what others will see when they do a search. Try it and see if you like what you read about yourself online.

There are two issues related to "your brand":

1. What you directly post about yourself, and

2. Potential posts that others tie to your name, "your brand".

What Tweets, Facebook photos and comments, Snapchats, and Instagrams are out there tied to your name, your brand? This is how serious this is; currently there are numerous attorneys, entrepreneurs and technology specialists who have developed businesses around "repairing" your brand. One example is called, reputationdefender. com. Do you want to have to pay someone to "repair" your brand or will you think before you post?

Complete a search of your name, "your brand" now and make notes of anything that you think could be interpreted negatively or incorrectly by someone who doesn't know you. Review and consider all sites where you typically post and what it says about who you are. Does your online presence provide the message you are seeking to share with the world? If you aren't currently using LinkedIn, review the functionality and consider how you can use LinkedIn to improve your brand persona.

Download the **My Brand Assessment Worksheet** from my website:m www.marchforwardconsulting.com or utilize the **My Brand Assessment Worksheet** in the Project of You Workbook.

As a second exercise: Download another **My Brand Assessment Worksheet** from my website: www.marchforwardconsulting.com or utilize the **My Brand Assessment Worksheet** in **The Project of You Workbook and** complete the **My Brand Assessment** for your accountability partner. Schedule a meeting to review and brainstorm and add SMART goals to your plans to make your brands as powerful and positive as you are.

"Your Personal Brand" is something that you will continue to grow and develop throughout your life. Schedule regular reviews of your online personal brand.

Remember that "You are what you post!". This is what the outside world learns about you.

Now that you have completed this Self Awareness key skill section, do you feel like you have more clarity about who you are and how you fit into the world?

Have you:

1. Learned whether you consider yourself as a specialist or multipotentialite?

2. Developed Your Mantra?

3. Determined what makes you happy?

4. Recognized the importance of your curiosity?

5. Learned to listen to your inner GPS?

6. Developed your personal brand?

If you cannot answer YES to all the questions above, go back and complete the unfinished exercises.

If you can answer all these questions with a YES, you are ready to march forward to the Connection and Communication Key skills for Success section with more clarity about you. As you work through the next section, the Connection key skills exercises, you will reference what you have discovered about what makes you happy and your natural curiosity to pick areas to explore further.

The Connection key skill is first because you can more clearly communicate who you are once you have discovered your connections. Having an increased awareness of yourself will benefit you as you begin to put yourself out there and define and develop your *Project of You Plan.* Being able to readily describe your traits, feelings and behaviors will enable you to sell yourself to a school or employer beyond high school.

CONNECTION

NOW THAT YOU have increased your self-awareness and discovered more about you, it's time to start making connections to decide how you will fit into the career world beyond high school. Remember your ultimate goal is to develop your *Project of You Plan* to become a happy, healthy, self-supporting adult.

In this concept section you will:

1. Discover your Why

2. Complete valuable research about your potential career paths

3. Learn about mentors and internships

4. Choose a hero

5. Review varied beyond high school paths

After completing the readings and exercises in this section, you will have stronger sense of your potential career and beyond high school paths, and that will make it easier to complete your *Project of You Plan* and march forward beyond high school.

WHY YOU DO WHAT YOU DO

WHERE YOU ARE going starts with what you do well…most of the time…but I agree with Simon Sinek - it starts with why you do what you do.

But my true hope for each of you is that you find your connection, your tribe, your WHY! I don't think anyone explains the importance of finding your why better than Simon Sinek. During his talk, he explains, "When we communicate from the inside out, we're talking directly to the part of the brain that controls behavior, and then we allow people to rationalize it with the tangible things we say and do.

This is where gut decisions come from. It's why you can give someone all the facts and figures and they'll say that they know what all the facts and the details say, but it just doesn't 'feel' right."

He describes the Wright Brothers story. It's an amazing insight into a historical perspective that will surprise you. There was another person you may never have heard of who was actually funded to develop our ability to fly.

Here is a portion of his TED talk:

Most people don't know about Samuel Pierpont Langley and back in the early 20th century, the pursuit of powered manned flight was like the dotcom of the day. Money was no problem. He held a seat at Harvard and worked at the Smithsonian and was extremely well connected. He hired the best minds money could find and the market conditions were fantastic. Then how come we have never heard of Samuel Pierpont Langley? A few hundred miles away in Dayton, Ohio lived Orville and Wilbur Wright. They had none of what we consider to be the recipe for success.

They had no money, they paid for their dream with the proceeds from their bicycle shop. Not a single person on the Wright brothers' team had a college education. Not even Orville or Wilbur. The difference was that Orville and Wilbur were driven by a cause, a purpose, a belief. They believed that if they could figure out this flying machine, it will change the course of the world.

Samuel Pierpont Langley wanted to be rich and famous. The people who believed in the Wright brothers' dream worked with them with blood, sweat, and tears. The others just worked for the paycheck. The Wright brothers would have to take five sets of parts because that's how many times they would crash before they came in for supper. And eventually on December 17, 1903 the Wright brothers took flight and no one was there to even experience it. We found out about it a few days later.

The day the Wright brothers took flight, Langley quit. He could have said, "That's an amazing discovery and I will improve upon your technology." But he didn't. He wasn't first, he didn't get rich, he didn't get famous, he quit. People don't buy what you do, they buy why you do it. And if you talk about what you believe, you will attract those who believe what you believe. Well, why is important to attract those who believe what you believe? "

The Wright brothers had no funding; just a desire, a curiosity, a drive, a WHY.

People don't buy what you do, they buy why you do it, and what you do is simply the proof, of what you believe. – Simon Sinek

Rather than add the entire transcript of his TED talk, I suggest you watch it; it's short - less than 20 minutes.

I love this TED talk. Check it out. It's enlightening: **Start With Why - Simon Sinek**

If you connect with what Simon describes in his talk, I would recommend his course, a different type of assessment. I've facilitated clients using Simon's Start with Why program and they felt they gained many insights.

But there are many other assessments you can utilize to assist you in learning more about you. I'm sure you have taken assessments either in school or online. What have they told you about your potential paths? Take the time to review your assessments and consider what you have learned about yourself from the data provided in the reports generated. Assessments are valuable tools to learn more about you and gain insights. I recommend taking any assessments offered to you. The more insights you have, the better.

As I mentioned at the beginning of the book, in some cases, it's important to work through these key skills for success with an objective, experienced coach or consultant. These tools will begin to provide insights for you but the collaboration will generate new ideas and paths for you. Bring your assessments with you to any sessions with a coach or counselor or review them with your accountability partner.

They are many great assessment tools such as:

MBTI,

Naviance,

What color is your parachute,

Career Liftoff Interest Inventory,

MAPP,

DISC,

Strength Finders,

360,

Birkman Method Assessment,

Start with Why,

and many others that you may discover in school or online.

I'm not going to go into a lot of detail regarding each assessment. As with foods, medicines, exercise, etc, there are varying opinions about what is best for you, and I do believe it's personal preference. Or possibly you decide based on what is offered to you by your school or your coach or counselor. Your coach or counselor will utilize what they believe is the most effective assessment to discover your best match for your future path. Each assessment can add some much needed insight into your unique genius. But in some cases, they can appear to be describing someone other than you depending on your level of self-awareness and self-perception. Assessments are great tools and in many cases, they can help you focus and gain insight. Your answers to the questions "who are you and what do you want to do beyond high school?" are still answers that you need to find within you.

These tools can help you focus and think about who you are and what you do well. You need to uncover why you do what you do. If you have completed an aptitude test, a core values inventory, and/or a personality inventory to better understand yourself, include them in your brainstorming and coaching sessions. All these components are part of your being and each will add to your success and enjoyment of any college choice, major choice and career choice. Just like a key fitting into a lock, everything must line up for you to feel truly engaged, empowered and energized by your daily work. If you already have an interest inventory, aptitude test, and/or personality inventory completed, these are a good place to start uncovering why you do what you do and what you do well.

The interesting part of utilizing this strategy for choosing things like a college major, college or university choice, or career is that having worked with many students and adults over the years, some people do NOT enjoy or feel rewarded by doing what they potentially do well according to some of these assessments. It's a potentially windy path to reach your perfect destination.

Most of you know who Steve Jobs is and what he accomplished. His Stanford commencement speech provides great insights into how you can "connect the dots" of your life to find your best fit.

Scott Dinsmore of Live Your Legend says:

Arguably the Best Career Guidance of All Time: My Favorite Talk by Steve Jobs

Written by SCOTT April 3, 2015

Watch Steve Jobs' speech by searching: Steve Jobs 2005 Stanford Commencement Speech

3 major take away key skills for success:

1. You can't connect the dots looking forward; you have to trust and have confidence to follow your heart

2. Keep looking - don't settle

3. Live each day as if it's the last day of your life

"Your time is limited, so don't waste it living someone else's life. Don't be trapped by dogma, which is living the results of other people's thinking. Don't let the noise of others' opinions drown out your own inner voice and most important, have the courage to follow your heart and intuition. They somehow already know what you truly already want to become. Everything else is secondary." Steve Jobs

I personally do believe that you will be drawn to the correct path for you eventually. But if you strive and make a dedicated effort to get to know yourself, it will be a destination that you reach sooner rather than later.

It's important to review and discuss these assessments in depth with a sounding board, like a coach, mentor, educational consultant, parent, guidance counselor or teacher to truly find your connection. Looking at the results in relation to how you feel, your current perception of yourself, your core values and your life goals will help you easily make choices about your future.

You owe it to yourself to truly know yourself! Find your connection and connect your dots looking back.

"Don't die with the music still in you."

~ Dr. Wayne Dyer

The thing to remember is that your choices have to fit you and what your aptitude tests show but there is also a strong need for connection. In most cases, people enjoy doing what they are great at because it gives them both a sense of accomplishment and a sense of winning, success, being on top. But in some cases, people find a connection to something that may not seem like it fits their aptitude.

I would also highly recommend reading

The Element: How Finding Your Passion Changes Everything.

by Sir Ken Robinson Ph.D.

I shared in the beginning of the book that Sir Ken Robinson is an English author, speaker and international advisor on education. If you aren't an avid reader, Sir Ken also has several TED talks for you to view.

He has many great examples in his book of people finding their passion, also referred to as their Why, their tribe, or their connection. When you find it, you know it. I have a colleague who is a coach and she was a corporate executive for years prior to becoming a coach. She said when she became part of the coaching community, "it was like stepping into a bath of warm water because it was so relaxing and comforting". She was so clear about her connection to coaching and her description was so vivid that I remember where we were when she shared that with me and I can still hear her words. It left a deep impact on me. I was at my first international coaching conference in Las Vegas. I went to learn more about the coaching profession and decide if it was the right next step. Listening to her description finalized my commitment to become a professionally certified coach. That is the feeling I want you to have about your *Project of You Plan*.

I have included a paraphrased synopsis of one example in Sir Ken's book below to give you a better idea of what reading his book will share with you.

Have you ever heard of someone making his or her career as a Science Comedian?

That is what Helen Pilcher has done. She at first thought she would be a Neuroscientist doing big experiments in a lab working with brain dissections and stem cells while wearing ridiculously unflattering safety specs but she changed her mind. She received the credentials needed to do that but she found that world was driven by business plans, and less motivated by curiosity. She realized that "I wanted to communicate science" and she further realized that she truly enjoyed performing comedy so she became a Science Comedian with a tag line of

"finding ways to make science groovy again".

Imagine going from planning to be a neuroscientist to a becoming a science comedian. But this worked for her. She found her tribe, her element, her connection and she is happy, healthy and self-supporting.

My hope is that you will stay curious and find your connection. It might require some creativity and some innovation to combine your interests or be willing to look at the world in your own new, unique way. Go for it! Be open to your possibilities!

I have shared another example below of someone you may know:

On a college tour at the University of Maryland, the guide shared that their most famous alum was Jim Henson, creator of the Muppets.

You likely know who I mean – The Muppets from Sesame Street and other TV shows and movies: Kermit, Miss Piggy, and the Electric Mayhem.

What our tour guide at University of Maryland shared was that Jim Henson had created his own major in puppetry while a student there.

This amazed me and inspired me and I hope it does you as well!

The Muppets (based on combining marionette and puppet) are now a common term but before Jim Henson, who knew that term?

Puppets weren't a new phenomena but a college major in puppetry surely was new.

Imagine what you might create if you left your mind open to the possibilities?

During high school, Jim Henson began creating puppets for a Saturday morning children's show. During college Henson continued creating puppets and producing puppet shows that were a financial success, but he began to have doubts about a career as a puppeteer. He explored in Europe for several months after college and was inspired by European puppeteers because it was a true art form there. Upon return to the US, he continued his puppetry career and the Muppets became a global brand.

Give yourself the time and opportunities to make your connections, find your why, and who knows what you might do, create, or invent in your future?

VALUABLE RESEARCH THAT
WILL LAST YOU A LIFETIME

THE TERM RESEARCH refers to extensive systematic investigation into a specific subject in order to discover facts about your subject. I'm sure you have read research reports or created research reports as part of your school curriculum. Now it's time to begin researching your potential path beyond high school. The more time and energy you give to your research, the greater chance you will choose a career, technical school, college major, gap year and/or college that are a fit for you.

The list of potential choices is infinite. That is why you need to do your research and narrow the list based on what you learned about yourself so far. Now that you better understand yourself by having defined:

- your mantra,
- what makes you happy,
- what makes you curious,
- whether you are a specialist or multipotentialite,
- and how to listen to your inner GPS,
- it's time to consider your why, your assessments and how you fit into your larger outer world.

You may have watched Shark Tank, where entrepreneurs bring their ideas to experts for advice and potential investing. There are so many ideas regarding how to support yourself as well as doing something rewarding when you start your career. The list of ideas and possibilities is virtually endless! I think that's what makes it so hard. There are too many choices and not enough time or information to decide without research and exploration. This is why discovering who you are, what you want to do and how to get there is so important. There is research that you can do to help narrow your list and match your personal traits with a potential college major or career area.

The reason this research is so important at this point in your life is because if you plan to attend a four-year college, an undergraduate degree is an expensive and time-consuming commitment. You will be committing four or more years and investing approximately $200,000 or more into your undergraduate degree. Going just because it's the next step without thinking about what you might eventually want to do with your life does not seem like a good investment or use of your time.

Putting the time in now will be worth its weight in gold to you. Getting an undergraduate degree in a field you are excited about and potentially starting your career in the direction you want or being prepared for graduate school if that is your choice is priceless. If your research tells you to wait or choose an alternative to college, again you have saved yourself lots of time and money, and that is always good news! Please don't take this lightly even though you aren't being graded on it!

To achieve great things, two things are needed; a plan, and not quite enough time.

~ Leonard Bernstein

While this may look like a large homework assignment, it's really not. Please don't feel overwhelmed. This process is invaluable and an important investment to make in yourself!

This will require some introspection from you and a few brief conversations with people you respect, admire, or have recently connected with, given they do something that intrigues you!

Here are your research steps - an important process. If you feel that you need assistance with any of these steps, reach out and ask for help from a mentor, coach, teacher, friend, counselor, educational consultant, or even your parents. Many parents and guardians are able to be great information sources but in some cases, students or parents and guardians feel the need to "let go" at this point. There is no right or wrong answer and using more than one resource may help you dig even deeper into your research. Everyone you work with brings their own personal experience to share with you.

I've listed some research steps below that are important to do as soon as you feel ready. I have worked with middle school students who were ready as well as high school students. These are also the same steps that my college student, young professional, midlife crisis, and career transition clients would complete to decide what is next for them if they haven't discovered it yet or if they simply are ready for a new challenge. Career transitions are not a negative thing. Many people simply decide that they want to challenge themselves to learn or do something new at some point in their lives. Just because you have been successful in a specific field doesn't mean you are locked in forever.

I know:

- former business people, engineers, and accountants who have become teachers because they had a desire,

- social work professionals who have become hairdressers and make-up artists because they wanted something more creative,

- engineers who have become fashion designers because it was something they always dreamed of and finally made it happen,

- pharmaceutical executives who have started a dog training business because they had a passion,

- teachers who have become floral designers because it was a passion,

- teachers who have started their own photography business because they loved it and wanted a more flexible schedule,

- photographers who have started their own jewelry line because it had been a lifelong dream and idea,

- nurse anesthetists who opened their own restaurant because they had the idea since middle school,

and these are just a few examples of the potential paths people I know have taken.

Download the **My Valuable Research Worksheet** from my website: www.marchforwardconsulting.com or utilize the **My Valuable Research Worksheet** in **The Project of You Workbook.**

Where do these intersect? You don't need to pick just one; perhaps the top three to five. You may love singing, finance, business, and event planning, so perhaps you will be a music manager rather than a performer? There are so many potential combinations but it may require some creativity, collaboration, and brainstorming to find your path.

After documenting your ideas and learning, work with your accountability partner, coach, mentor, parent or guidance counselor.

Download the **My Research Review Worksheet** from my website: www.marchforwardconsulting.com or utilize the **My Research Review Worksheet** in **The Project of You Workbook.**

You don't have to stop researching after completing your first three interviews; keep going and learn all you can. Gaining knowledge and insight will empower you to make the best plan for you and be prepared for your future beyond high school.

Keep exploring and document your findings in your Project of You folder. Take the answers to your Research Review questionnaire and decide how you can become more of an expert in the areas that interest you.

Are there:

- course electives in your school,
- college level courses,
- community night school classes,
- lectures in your community,
- non-profit organizations that offer volunteer opportunities,
- TED talks on the subject,
- online courses ,
- summer exploration camps,
- internship opportunities,
- job shadow opportunities,
- local SCORE events, or
- gap year programs in your area of interest?

There is no one else responsible to find those opportunities for you; you need to be an explorer and find them. They are out there and they do exist for many areas of interest. It may not seem easy to find them. They may not be on a bulletin board in your school or in your email, but you can find them if you " dig deeper" and explore and search.

Why dig deeper? Ask Taylor.

I recently spoke with Taylor, a recent college grad. She was a student athlete and chose her university based on being asked to play division one lacrosse there as well as to major in exercise science and become a physical therapist. As a student athlete in a "rough" sport, she was famil-iar with physical therapy as a patient and found it interesting.

Taylor enjoyed her college years both playing lacrosse and academically. During school she did part time internships in physical therapy but also became interested in cardiac rehabilitation. During her last semester she was required to do a full time/12 credit internship. She was fortunate to find a cardiac rehabilitation internship at a local hospital. During her internship she met many health care workers with varied titles. Taylor maximized her internship by asking many questions of her co-workers.

She began digging deeper and learning more about her options beyond college. Taylor discovered that rather than going to graduate school for physical therapy, she really wanted to become a PA – physician's assistant because it would offer her many more varied opportunities. Taylor fur-ther realized that she had a true interest in medicine and overall health. She wanted to study and do work in areas beyond physical therapy. Her time at the hospital was invaluable to allow her to dig deeper and fully explore all options for a career in healthcare. During that time, she considered following her physical therapy path, cardiac rehabilitation, nursing, PA (Physician's Assistant), and medical doctor.

Taylor is certain now that she wants to go to graduate school to become a PA. She expressed to me that she wished she had done more exploring and dug deeper as a high school student. Taylor believes that if she had done similar exploration as a high school student, she would have had a shorter timeframe and less expensive path to becoming a PA. Her undergraduate and perhaps even her high school class choices may have been different had she known that was her plan. Taylor also feels that she may have chosen a different undergraduate school, one that had a PA program. None of us know for sure what we would have done looking back, but Taylor and I both know that research and experience is always valuable. And she now will continue to dig deeper to achieve her goals, as she is clear about the next steps in her Project of You Plan.

Download the **My Dig Deeper Plan Worksheet** from my website: www.marchforwardconsulting.com or utilize the **My Dig Deeper Plan Worksheet** in your **The Project of You Workbook.**

Don't limit yourself to the categories listed, and add anything else you or your accountability partner can think of to enhance your knowledge and gain experience.

After completing the My Dig Deeper Plan Worksheet, prioritize your list and create SMART goals for the top three within the next two months.

We study history to learn from our mistakes, right? And many of the inhabitants of the US are here now because Columbus was ready to explore and sailed here from another continent. There have been numerous explorers and inventors throughout history who have changed the course of their lives as well as others' lives by "digging deeper" to make a discovery. Imagine if Tim Berners – Lee had not invented the Internet - you would function totally differently in your world than you do now in so many ways. For one, I personally would hate to go back to reading hard copy maps to find directions to a new place. Think about how many times a day you access the Internet and if it didn't exist? Life without Google Maps, or Waze or Uber is unimaginable now that they exist.

Now we can be connected to almost anyone almost anywhere in the world because of the changes available in technology. The game is constantly changing, and there is no defined finite list of jobs that you can do to fulfill yourself and support yourself as an adult. Given technology and innovation, new careers are being defined everyday. Jobs that people may have had to do in the past are going away because so many functions can be automated. You need to be an explorer! Or call it a researcher if you don't want to put yourself in the same category as Dora.

Think outside the box; don't limit yourself to careers that you already know about. Consider problems or concerns that you have and how they could potentially be solved. Think about the ideas that you have had, ideas to improve your life or someone else's or the world, no matter how far fetched, and write them down.

As you are exploring be sure to write your thoughts and ideas down; keeping them in your head won't help you to eventually connect the dots. To connect your dots, you will need to see what you have learned and share it with others to brainstorm the possibilities. Collaboration with others can produce ideas that may not have happened if you are working individually. Collaboration is a significant part of your exploration.

You never know what your ideas will be worth monetarily, inspirationally, clinically, innovatively, or just for your own personal fulfillment. Leave your legacy; your ideas might help someone else in a way that you can't envision right now.

Below is a story about a famous song that is inspirational. I'm hoping it will motivate you to write your ideas and research and exploration findings down and keep them in your Project of You folder.

Will you write something worth $422,500.00 someday?

The hand-written lyrics of Bob Dylan's song "The times they are a changing" (written on a napkin) sold at auction at Sotheby's, New York, for $422,500.00.

Do you think you should be writing your thoughts & ideas down?

I definitively say yes!

*One of my quotes from my book chapter in the **Women's Guide to Self – Esteem** is:*

> **"Putting your intentions into writing gives them a life of their own, even if it's on a napkin!"**
> **~ Brenda Jo March**

So take the time to put your thoughts into writing, in a:

- to do list,

- project plan,

- book chapter,

- reminder to call a friend,

- text/email to yourself,

- calendar update,

- journal entry, or

- note on that tablet next to your bed.

With all our new technology tools, there are so many ways to collect and initiate your thoughts into an action. Find what works best for you and stick to it. The key is to get your ideas out of your head and documented. Many people tell me they don't need to write things down because they will remember and many do but if you don't, what then?

Something potentially valuable that your brilliant brain thought for a brief moment may be permanently lost. If that never crosses your mind again, what will happen to that brilliant idea! Think if Dylan hadn't written these lyrics down; would they ever have become the amazing, timeless song that they are now? And the lyrics are still so valid even in our world today.

Steve Jobs recited the first line of this song as his opening when he unveiled the Macintosh in 1984, 21 years after the song was written. For those of you who know the song, you know what I mean and if you don't know it, it's worth a listen!

Dylan's first performance at the White House was 46 years after he took the time to write the lyrics for this inspiring song!

My favorite line from the song is:

"Come mothers and fathers

Throughout the land

And don't criticize

What you can't understand"

We all need to learn compassion - not criticism. We don't always understand another's perspective but that doesn't make it wrong.

There are many people who could potentially offer you advice and insight as you plan your future. Career exploration workshops are also a great option. If your school doesn't offer career exploration workshops, request that workshops be offered and ask your parents and guardians to make the same request to the school. Or look for workshops online or in your area. Be open to all possibilities for research and exploration.

In a time of turbulence and change, it is more true than ever that knowledge is power. President John F. Kennedy

If you need or want more personalized assistance and accountability, you can hire a personal coach, mentor or educational consultant to assist you. If cost is an issue, many coaches and consultants offer group sessions like I do that are more cost effective. In many cases, learning through your interactions with others sparks collaboration and new ideas.

No matter what you do, put some time and energy into this research and exploration It's YOUR *Project of You Plan*, YOUR life and as Bon Jovi sings in his song, "My Life":

"It's my life

It's now or never

I ain't gonna live forever!"

For additional inspiration and a great reminder that anything is possible,

watch Scott Dinsmore "s TED talk, "How to Find & Do Work You Love"

Scott is the creator of "Live Your Legend - Change the world by doing work you love"

DO YOU WANT A MENTOR?

WHAT IS A mentor? A mentor is a person willing to teach or give help and advice to a less experienced person. Generally a mentor is chosen because of their expertise in your field of interest or because they have achieved a goal similar to your goal.

Once you decide on your beyond high school path, being mentored by an experienced adult in your future industry will help you make the best choices to march forward. A great mentor can also guide you and help you make the connections needed for success. Consider who could be a great mentor for you and begin making a brief list of what you request from them as far as guidance and assistance. Respect their time, do your research and be prepared for your potential discussions with them.

In most cases, a great mentor is someone you need to seek out and request their help. As with everything in life, sometimes you get lucky and the right mentor happens to cross your path.

Download the **My Mentor Worksheet** from my website: www.marchforwardconsulting.com or utilize the **My Mentor Worksheet** in **The Project of You Workbook.**

After completing the Mentor worksheet, prioritize your list and create SMART goals for the top three within the next two months.

Below is a story of one of my clients who found a mentor without actually trying and she learned a lot!

Do you have an official or unofficial mentor or coach?

I would like to share a story about Liz She is a college graduate from a "good" school with a marketable major and has an interesting, lucrative first job. It is her first job out of college and she hasn't been there a year yet. Liz is living my mantra of what we all need – HHSS – Happy, Healthy and Self-supporting, all any of us truly need to focus on as our outcome. Liz reminded me why I have this dream.

I have the dream to see every high school, university, and organization offer coaching and mentoring to its students and employees.

So I'd like to share our discussion as it brings out a great point.

Liz has been trying to decide on her next move as far as her career is concerned. Her commitment in her current role is for a year, and then she can choose another role to learn more about the company and also herself in the process. She had been offered an exciting new position reporting to a dynamic, positive director. It sounded perfect for her and she was ready to accept that as her next position, but then life happened and she made a new discovery and was open to the possibility.

Liz had formed a relationship with another superior in a restaurant in the evening after a conference outside of work. They bonded over discussions about music, "great but obscure guitar players", as a starter. This of course led to discussions about bands and songs. They were both amazing, true music fans, and true fans can talk all night about that amazing rift or great lyric or how a certain vocal makes you feel or songs during which you can't sit down, and that the energy of music is never ending and a true connecting force! So a friendship was created; a bond was formed out of mutual respect for another music lover. Both persons also saw the other as someone fun, dynamic and interesting. This occurred because of and in spite of their love for music. The conversation naturally led to current challenges in the workplace and many interesting topics were covered.

What 3 things do you do better than anyone else?

Fast forward several weeks and they have an official meeting at the office

119

to discuss her career path. This superior had seen a spark in her and was unofficially coaching and mentoring her. What an unexpected gift! He wanted to help her hone in on her talents and gifts to be able to make the best decision for her next step in her career path, and so he asked her an inspired question.

"What are the 3 things that you do better than anyone else in the world?"

Liz was stumped. And she is not a person who doesn't typically have an answer on the tip of her tongue, believe me. So this bothered her. He suggested that she find the answer to that question and always have it on the tip of her tongue in the future. He had given her excellent unsolicited advice that she could utilize for the rest of her life.. This was a true gift to her. So she is searching for her strengths so that she can verbalize them whenever she is asked that question.

Were you raised not to brag? You need to learn to share your strengths.

The lessons you may have been taught about not bragging and being boastful and thinking of others are valid. But those lessons are also a hindrance to you achieving self-awareness combined with humility. Successful people are able to share their strengths but still maintain a sense of humility. If someone directly asks you your strengths, there is nothing wrong with being to spout your strengths off as easily as flipping a light switch on.

Do you know your strengths? Can you spout them out in a New York minute if asked?

If yes, that is great! If no, it's time to spend some time thinking, meditating, being still and figuring it out. You may also need to find a mentor to assist and inspire you to find some clarity around your strengths and where you want to go with them.

So you were fortunate to find a mentor? What if this is not the case?

There is another aha lesson for me from this moment in time. I was thrilled to see the unofficial mentoring happening in a small microcosm of a large corporation. But I also wondered if it would have happened if my client were not a demonstrative, expressive, strong communicator who exudes joy in discussing music. Would that connection have formed if she were a naturally shy, introverted soul? Perhaps not/ So how do you find a mentor if you are shy or introverted?

If you are shy and introverted, it would be beneficial for you to work on your "connecting, relationship building" skills to connect with others to create more opportunities for yourself.

The time spent on learning connecting techniques and perfecting your "gift of gab" around your interests will be invaluable. It's amazing how fulfilling your personal, "outside of work" hobbies are and how sharing them is even better. Your hobbies and interests can deepen your ability to connect with others. Whether it's music, movies, food, wine, art, theatre, video games, fashion, interior design, dance, travel, or any other ways you enjoy life and express your individuality, finding someone else who enjoys something you also love is an amazing connector. The key is being open, passionate, and authentic, and learning it's ok to "share yourself".

If you feel you need practice, role-play and practice your networking skills with your accountability partner, coach, or a trusted friend.

It's not an easy skill for everyone.

Liz exudes positive energy but she feels it is actually hard for her to "put herself out there". After high school, being away at college and during internships, she pushed herself beyond her comfort zone to put herself out there. Why? Because after pushing herself, she learned it works and so she has worked to develop these skills.

Liz shared with me that she has friends who didn't push themselves, and they have struggled with internships and in job hunting. You may have a great deal to offer but are not necessarily easily drawn out? How can another person discover your brilliance, if you aren't willing to share you? Whenever you have the opportunity, take the time to connect with someone who is new to you, build your "easy connector" personality type, and take advantage of the experience. You might find a mentor in the process or perhaps spark a new idea for you or your colleague. Helping others discover their unique gifts is the greatest gift that we can give them and also a gift to ourselves.

The people who mentor you often make just one request in return - that you mentor someone else in the future when you are ready.

Seeing the light go on in another person and seeing them grow and thrive is like Master Card - "priceless"!

WHO ARE YOUR HEROES?

THE DEFINITION OF a hero is a person admired for bravery, great achievements, or good qualities. In some cases a hero might be the main character of a story, movie, or play. Perhaps you think of someone you know who has overcome many obstacles as your hero? In fact, the person you chose as your mentor may be your hero. Sometimes you need to find your heroes; they aren't all in the news regularly. Sure, if your hero is a rock star, politician or professional athlete, most everyone knows them but there are many "unsung" heroes and if you find yours, it may help you to craft your inner hero!

Seth Godin wrote an amazing manifesto on Education entitled *Stop Stealing Dreams*. I highly recommend everyone read it to consider the changes that could be made in education. Below is a study done with surprising results. This is an excerpt from Seth's manifesto:

Jake Halpern did a rigorous study of high school students. The most disturbing result was this: "When you grow up, which of the following jobs would you most like to have?"

The chief of a major company like General Motors A Navy SEAL A United States Senator

The president of a great university like Harvard or Yale

The personal assistant to a famous singer or movie star

The results:

Among girls, the results were as follows: 9.5 percent chose "the chief of a major company like General Motors"; 9.8 percent chose "a Navy SEAL"; 13.6 percent chose "a United States Senator"; 23.7 percent chose "the president of a great university like Harvard or Yale"; and 43.4 percent chose "the personal assistant to a famous singer or movie star."

Notice that these kids were okay with not actually being famous—they were happy to be the assistant of someone who lived that fairy tale lifestyle.

Is this the best we can do? Have we created a trillion-dollar, multi-million- student, sixteen-year schooling cycle to take our best and our brightest and snuff out their dreams—sometimes when they're so nascent that they haven't even been articulated? Is the product of our massive schooling industry an endless legion of assistants?

The century of dream-snuffing has to end. We're facing a significant emergency, one that's not just economic but cultural as well. The time to act is right now, and the person to do it is you.

After reading Seth's manifesto excerpt above, consider what it would take for you to find a hero of your own. Think about the results of your areas of interest and find successful heroes in those areas. They may not be on TV or YouTube regularly, may not have a reality show or be inducted into a hall of fame, but I'm sure there are people doing amazing things everywhere in every line of work. With all the information so readily available to you, with a little research, you can find your historic or modern day hero.

Think about it and search out your heroes, learn their stories and their paths, and consider in what ways you can emulate them! Just as an example I've added a list of the top 10 inventors of all time; perhaps one of them is your hero? This list below is from the biogra-phyonline.net site.

Thomas Edison (1847 – 1931) Edison filed over 1,000 patents. He developed and innovated a wide range of products from the electric light bulb to the phonograph and motion picture camera.

The Wright Brothers – Successfully designed, built and flew the first powered aircraft, showing that man could fly. This was one of most important inventions of the Twentieth Century.

Benjamin Franklin (1705 – 1790) He was a Polymath who discovered electricity and invented the Franklin stove.

Nikola Tesla (1856 –1943) Serbian born scientist who immigrated to the US. He was a brilliant scientist who played a key role in the development of AC electricity – through the AC induction motor, transformer, and Tesla coil. His method of AC electricity has been the template for global electricity use.

Charles Babbage (1791 – 1871) Created the first mechanical computer, which proved to be the prototype for future computers. He was considered to be the 'Father of Computers'.

James Watt (1736 – 1819) Inventor of the steam engine, which was critical in the industrial revolution. His invention of a separate condensing chamber greatly improved the efficiency of steam.

Alexander Bell (1847 – 1922) Credited with inventing the first practical telephone. Also worked on optical telecommunications, aeronautics and hydrofoils.

Leonardo Da Vinci (1452 – 1519) One of the greatest ever minds, he invented models that proved workable 3-500 years later.

Galileo (1564-1642) Developed a powerful telescope and confirmed revolutionary theories about the nature of the world. He also developed an improved compass.

Tim Berners Lee - Developed the http:// protocol for the internet and made the world wide web freely available.

In addition to these historic heroes, many of you may think of these few well- known modern day successful entrepreneurs like:

Steve Jobs – Apple

Mark Zuckerberg – Facebook

Warren Buffet – Berkshire Hathaway

Tony Robbins – Personal Coaching

Bill Gates – Microsoft

Arianna Huffington – Huffington Post

Sarah Blakely – Spanx

Oprah Winfrey – Harpo Productions

as your potential heroes. Of course there are many heroes in numerous other fields, such as people who:

- have made medical discoveries that saved lives Like Jonas Salk, or
- have helped bring peace between communities like Nelson Mandela, or
- have created amazing works of literature like William Shakespeare, or
- have stood up for what they believed in and righted a wrong like Rosa Parks and Jackie Robinson

Of course the list is endless and it is your personal choice to perceive a person as your hero.

But considering and choosing one or more personal heroes can be an inspiration for you as you move forward. If you learn most of your potential heroes' back-stories (where they came from, what they were given and how they reached their goals), you will find that in most cases, it wasn't an easy road to achieve what they achieved. Your heroes' back stories can motivate you to not give up if reaching your goal becomes difficult. And your hero doesn't have to be a famous or historical figure. I've met students who chose a parent, teacher, relative or neighbor who was a hero in their eyes. You are creating connections and intentions both in your mind and with the outside world.

Download the **Who is My Hero Worksheet** from my website: www.marchforwardconsulting.com or utilize the **Who is My Hero Worksheet** in **The Project of You Workbook.**

YOU DON'T KNOW WHAT YOU WANT UNTIL YOU TRY IT?

AGAIN, GOING BACK to the food learning analogy earlier in the book, you only learn by actually trying something. Now that you have researched your potential career paths, it is time to take a risk by trying something new and gaining experience. You can do this by finding an internship, doing a job shadow, or scheduling an informational interview. Do something you haven't done before; push yourself beyond your comfort zone.

You don't need to wait for an ad to be posted that an internship or job shadow opportunity exists to make it happen for you. Decide what type of experience you want based on what you learned during your valuable research. Consider the types of experiences that you feel would be most beneficial. Reach out to people you know and trust and let them know what you are seeking and ask for their assistance. Use your current connections to your advantage to create new ones. If you feel that you need help getting started, go to my website and download **the Connection Request Template** that you can adapt to your specific needs.

Who or what is more important to you than your future success?

What are you doing to enhance your education or career?

Whether you are 13 or 17 or 23, it's up to you to find and create moments of growth in your education. Don't wait for a teacher, friend, or mentor to encourage you to improve your skills to guarantee your own success. Many students assume that they will have a myriad of opportunities to gain necessary skills as part of college courses, internships, and early career positions. And that is a true possibility. There are many wonderful companies out there that are committed to employee development. While I agree that having an active social life is an important part of being young, there is time for both. Many of the classes, workshops, and seminars available now are delivered in group settings and can also be a fun social activity.

Why not get started now? What are you waiting for?

I work with young professionals as well as mature professionals daily who are frustrated by their lack of growth, challenge, and personal development within their current company. If you want to find them, there are a myriad of online, in-person, individual and group training classes and workshops in any of the "soft skills" or "technical skills" that you want to be able to add to your resume. You may be assuming you are getting everything you need in your academic classes, but there is always room for enhancing and improving your skills and gaining much needed real world career experience. Try something new - seek out opportunities to gain the skills needed to be ready to hit the ground running when you get out of school.

Who or what is more important to you than your future success?

> *" This is your time here to do what you must do"*
>
> *~ John Mellencamp's song, "Your Life is Now"*

Why my intern approached me at 14?

I realized by watching my own children who were introduced to technology by middle school age that just as learning a foreign language, the earlier you introduce technology the easier it is to learn. So it made perfect sense to have an intern both to discuss how students perceive ideas as well as to assist with technology projects.

The Downingtown Area school district is committed to adding experiential learning as much as possible at the secondary level and offered to run an ad for an intern for my business. I had 4 students respond: 2 juniors, 1 senior and 1 freshman. After speaking to them all on the phone, I was surprised that the freshman sounded the most prepared and the best fit. She is mature, has a great outlook, and is open to all possibilities. She recognized what a new experience could offer her. Whatever you learn both in formal academic training as well as in experiential learning can never be taken away from you; it's all positive growth for your future.

Here is Olivia's summary written in her own words of why she approached me and what she feels she learned.

I came to acquire an internship with Brenda March at March Forward Consulting through my high school's career center. It was posted on the morning announcements that there was an opportunity to intern with a woman who needed assistance with creating and operating social media accounts for her business. I immediately jumped at the offer, considering I had been looking for an internship or job at the time, and am reasonably skilled with the use of social media. I talked to Mrs. Wick, the career center advisor, and she connected me to Brenda via email. Brenda and I then talked on the phone about prospective opportunities of an internship, and what responsibilities I would have. By the time we finished up our conversation, I had already realized how great an opportunity this could turn out to be.

Since then, I have had many roles in March Forward Consulting of varying responsibilities. I've been mainly involved in the Young Empowered Speakers Program. I have written blogs on public speaking and related topics that were sent out to the students in the program, as well as coming to the meetings and helping out in general. Also, I helped to create the social media pages of Brenda's website, C-ing Success. Other than that, I've done work here and there such as drafting emails and typing up release forms. The biggest project that I've taken on with Brenda is a book about education that we are co-authoring along with several others. I am in the process of writing a chapter on the experience aspects of school that aren't primarily academic. The book will hopefully start coming together in the next couple months, and I can't wait to see it published somewhere. To have the opportunity to be a published author at the age of 15 is something I could never have dreamed of.

A big skill I've come to utilize from working with Brenda is time management. I have been able to better balance my life. I did face the difficulty of figuring out my scheduling with this internship, but to be honest I expected this from the beginning. She and I are both busy people, so it's sometimes hard to find a time to work together that works for both of us. However, when push comes to shove, we always make it work for each other. Also, I've learned a lot about professionalism. There's a lot of pressure in knowing that someone is depending on you, not just to get a good grade or do a small favor, but to accomplish something that is important to his or her business. On the other hand, this pressure is somewhat empowering. It feels great to know that somebody has enough faith in you to give you greater responsibilities in a business.

I definitely think this internship has prepared me for the future. I know how difficult it is to do some of the things professionals do, but I also know that those things are much easier if you enjoy them. Through this experience I have come to further understand my love for writing, which has pushed my motivation to pursue it as a career in some form. Anything that you can do to get a better grip on what you have a passion for in life is something that is worth your time. Sometimes these things cross ideas off the list, and sometimes they highlight ones of interest. Luckily for me, my experience with Brenda has certainly highlighted some interests of mine.

— *Olivia Hunt*

THERE IS NO MAGIC ANSWER...
MAYBE TAKE AN ALTERNATIVE PATH?

THERE ARE SO many paths to take beyond high school so don't assume that the only path is directly to a four year college which is what many students do assume. If you know what you want to do with your life and it requires a four - year degree, that may be your answer but many successful people have chosen alternative paths based on various factors such as:

- You already have a business started that you want to grow.
- You want to get some type of technical training.
- You want to gain more experience and self -awareness.
- You don't feel ready for college either because you don't know what you want to do or you don't believe you have the self-discipline to succeed.
- Or you are not willing to accrue debt.

There are many other alternatives than immediately heading from high school to college. College is an expensive endeavor and not the answer for everyone out of the gate. Life is not about doing what you should or have to in a situation. But there are the basic safety rules and having consideration for yourself and others. The growth that can be obtained by experiential learning is immeasurable whether via a job, internship, volunteer position, a formal Gap Year program, or perhaps even a combination of part time college courses and some other form of experiential learning.

As you learned in the valuable research worksheet, the key is to know what you want and doing the research to find a perfect match for your *Project of You Plan*. There are numerous ways to reach your goal immediately following high school:

- 4 year college,

- work and take courses online,

- do a GAP year,

- get a certification at a technical school,

- begin a paid internship,

- take a year off and gain work experience,

- start your own business,

- go to college part time initially and do further career exploration, or some other combination for your plan.

I'm going to share four alternative key skills for success to traditional four-year college beyond high school path.

1. Start your career now

2. Plan a Gap Year like Malia Obama

3. Get an Associate degree at a Community college

4. Try a technical school

I will give you a few things to consider about each option and then you can add your thoughts and ideas about any alternatives that feel right to you on your plan materials.

Download the **Pro/Con Worksheet** from my website: www.marchforwardconsulting.com or utilize the **Pro/Con Worksheet** in **The Project**

of You Workbook to help you make your final decision. The Pro/Con Worksheet is a great tool to use whenever you are faced with a tough choice, and feel free to use it for any other decisions you may be trying to make in your future.

Start your career now

If you feel that you are ready for the working world and know what you want to do, starting your career immediately after high school is an option. Dependent on the training and job experience that you received during your high school years, perhaps you already have a career plan. If you worked for an organization during high school and they offered to have you work for them full-time once you graduate, that is your decision. Consider the experience you have gained working there as you decide and whether or not you feel it is the best plan for you to continue on there. Also learn more about the industry you are working in - is this an industry with growth and potential for you in your future? Can you see a possible path of advancement for you in this industry?

If you decide to go immediately to work after high school, think about more than the salary and the title. When seeking a new position, ask about what types of support they have for employee development? How would they describe the corporate culture? Research the organization's financial history. It's your job to interview them as much as the reverse, to decide if it is a good fit for you.

It's a valid concern if you want to work for financial reasons because you feel the cost of college will be a financial burden to you. Ask your employer if they have a tuition reimbursement plan; it's another way to complete your degree without accruing debt. There are many options for completing your college courses such as test-out programs, online classes, and credit for life experience that you can also potentially research and utilize. Depending on your area of interest, a four-year degree may or may not be necessary. Research and know what is recommended for your chosen industry and develop your *Project of You Plan* based on what you feel is the best path for your future.

Plan a Gap Year like Malia Obama

What is a Gap Year? During "a Gap Year" students can take "one year to travel, pursue a special project or activity, or work or spend time in another meaningful way". A Gap Year is encouraged by many schools, and one example is Harvard. Malia Obama was accepted to Harvard but will defer her admission for a year and pursue other enriching experiences. The Gap Year is not unique to Harvard but if you are considering a Gap Year, research the policy at your potential college or university as not all colleges and universities will allow it.

Harvard is one of the more than 5 percent of four-year institutions that allow admitted students to defer their admission for a year without penalty, as reported by *the Wall Street Journal*. Gap years have been popular in Europe and now participation in these programs is increasing in the US. Overall in the US, it is still a small percentage of students who choose a Gap year. Many come from high-income families as they tend to be expensive but now some colleges have been offering financial aid packages for accepted Gap Year deferred students.

To give you some examples of possible Gap Year activities, this is an excerpt from Harvard's website:

Some options for the interim year

Members of one recent class participated in the following activities, and more, in the interim year: drama, figure skating, health-care, archeological exploration, kibbutz life, language study, mineralogical research, missionary work, music, non-profit groups, child welfare programs, political campaigns, rebuilding schools, special needs volunteering, sports, steel drumming, storytelling, swing dance, university courses, and writing—to name some chosen at random. They took their interim year in the following locales: Belize, Brazil, China, Costa Rica, Denmark, Ecuador, France, Germany, Guatemala, Honduras, India, Ireland, Israel, Italy, Mongolia, Nepal, Philippines, Scandinavia, Scotland,

Spain, Switzerland, Taiwan, Thailand, Uruguay, United States and Zimbabwe.

Many students divide their year into several segments of work, travel, or study. Not all can afford to travel or to take part in exotic activities. A number have served in the military or other national service programs. Some remain at home, working, taking part-time courses, interning, and still finding the time to read books they have never had time to fit into their schedules or begin to write the "great American novel." Others have been able to forge closer ties with parents or grandparents from whom they may have drifted away during the hectic pace of the high-school years.

What is the advantage of your potential Gap Year?

Many educators and students feel that a student who takes a gap year enters college more energized and focused and more mature. In many cases, their Gap Year experiences help students feel more certain about their major choice. Or in some cases, they know what they don't want to do and ruling out is as important as ruling in - both provide lifetime learning. The Gap Year is not for everyone, so research it fully if this is an option you choose to consider.

Mandi Schmitt, the public relations and special projects director at Go Overseas, an international program review site in Berkeley, California, said the industry is still struggling with its reputation.

She further writes: After the princes in the UK took Gap Years, participation increased. Europe and Australia consider the Gap Year a productive option. Some Americans view it as irresponsible, lazy and kind of the counter to doing a responsible four-year institution, per Mandi Schmitt. Malia Obama's decision to take time o before Harvard could make a big impact. Gap- year clients are generally young and depend on their wary parents to approve of — and fund — their activities. e fact that the president of the U.S. is allowing his daughter to take a gap year will likely go a long way, just as it did with the British royals, Schmitt said.

"Even just reading the news, hearing the word 'gap year' helps parents be more comfortable with it," she said.

These sorts of changing attitudes could help destigmatize gap years as well.

Another potential advantage is that gaining experience working or volunteering in an area such as career development, medical assistance, legal advice, or any other potential direction you choose will be a great addition to your resume. If you choose to travel and work in another country, you will also gain a unique perspective on another country and its culture and people. Given the global economy, this experience is invaluable. A Gap Year experience can help prepare you for your career by being an opportunity for vital exposure in your chosen industry.

There are numerous Gap Year planning programs online and locally. Do your homework and check out the options online as well as at your future intended college or university before making a decision. It's an option to consider but make sure you research all aspects of the cost, benefit and time involved before making that type of decision.

Get an Associate degree at a Community college

Another alternative to a four-year college or university is starting out at a community college or doing an online program and starting out with a plan to obtain a two-year associate degree. This gives you the option to be exposed to college and learn more about who you are and what you want. Most community colleges and online universities are less expensive than the four-year programs so it will save you money. If you decide to go on and work towards a four-year degree, most community colleges have relationships with four-year programs so marching forward to complete your bachelor's degree is possible if you choose that path. Completing your Associate degree shows potential future employers that you can make a commitment and stick to it. Any opportunities for education and experience are an opportunity to grow and expand your network and your resume.

Try a technical school

There are numerous technical schools - everything from dental assistant to HVAC technician to massage therapist. If you have an interest in any of these fields, it's a way to invest less time and money than in most four-year college programs. In addition, many of the technical schools provide hands on training during your program and assistance in job placement upon completion of your program. There are always needs for people in the many trades that provide training within a technical school. Many students feel they must get their four-year degree immediately following high school. In speaking to a colleague who is a recruiter at a technical school, she said they rarely recruit at local high schools because in their area, most high school students feel college is the best answer. For many people it is but for others, taking a non-traditional routes is best.

One real world example is Laura. Laura went to college and received a bachelor's degree in social work and worked in the field but always wanted something more creative and hands on. Eventually she went back to beauty school and now enjoys doing hair and make-up. Laura said she is happy with both her choices but in hindsight would have gone straight to beauty school if she didn't feel college was a requirement. Laura further stated that she would not have incurred the college debt if she had originally seen beauty school as an option.

For those of you who are considering this as a path but would also like to eventually earn your degree, it's useful to know that many people make that choice also.

As an example, one successful entrepreneur that I know, Krista, originally went to beauty school and immediately started working as a beautician. She was able to readily support herself upon beauty school graduation and her parents were able to pay her beauty school tuition without going into debt. While she was enjoying her career, she wanted to expand her horizons and decided that she wanted to learn more about business so she went back to school part time and eventually earned a business degree. Since that time, she has opened her own salon and employs several other beauticians. Krista has not only achieved being a successful beautician but also a successful entrepreneur running her own business.

You have to do what is right for you but don't discount going to a technical school if it interests you. Being certified in a skill or trade is something you can always utilize to support yourself even if you make a career change at some point in the future. Like Krista, you can always go back and get your college degree later if you feel that you want to learn a skill or trade now and start earning a living. You have to own it; no one will tell you what to do.

> ***By failing to prepare, you are preparing to fail.***
> **~ Benjamin Franklin**

My friend and colleague Tom Sterner writes in his book, *The Practicing Mind,*

> **"None of us learn anything except through our own direct experiences".**

This is so true and as a parent or friend, we want to download our "life lessons" to others but this is not possible. There is no standard or magic formula that suits any individual. The beauty of the world is that we are all unique individuals with varied interests, strengths, desires, and passions. Finding your path to being your best unique self and living your passion can be difficult when you combine it with worrying about obtaining a college degree to be able to support yourself in the style that you have grown accustomed to with your family.

There are many logistical considerations as far as timing, budget, and value of the opportunity that you create for yourself. There are several formal Gap Year planning organizations and in many cultures, a gap year is fairly standard. If you are interested in trying to develop an "out of the box" approach to planning your first year post high school, seek a professional who can help. An experienced coach or consultant can help you develop a plan that aligns with your true values and passions. Discover what you really want and make a constructive, realistic plan to take the next step.

No one else knows exactly who you are or what you feel. While parents and guardians and teachers may want the best for you, there is always the chance that you aren't able to easily articulate with them what you really want. This is a valuable lesson for a parent - as your child becomes the young adult they were meant to be, the parent doesn't know how it feels to be that child. When I hear these words from **Tom Petty, " *You don't know how it feels to be me*",** it's a great reminder. You need to remember that no one else can understand how you feel unless you share with him or her exactly how you feel. No one is a mind reader. So while your parents and guardians may love and know you well, they don't know how it feels to be you and cannot guide you unless you can express what you want.

The answers lie within each of you and sometimes it takes an objective third party to help draw them out. Being able to share how you feel and what you want confidently is the greatest gift you can give yourself and your parents and guardians as well as your teachers, mentors, and coaches. The people who want to help you find your way will be able to assist you better if you can verbalize what you want.

"It wasn't a book that changed my life; it was a writer." *"Almost from the moment that David asked whether he would emerge as the hero of his own life, a notion that hadn't yet occurred to me, I was in."*

Anna Quindlen The book that changed my life was David Copperfield by Charles Dickens. AARP Feb/March 2016

Download the **Pro/Con of College Alternatives Worksheet** from my website: www.marchforwardconsulting.com or utilize the **Pro/Con of College Alternatives Worksheet** in **The Project of You Workbook.**

What is your individual dream/vision?

We are all amazing individuals with unique individual gifts that in most cases can't be measured by tests, GPA's, SAT's, statistics, etc. If each of us truly locked into what we believe we can be or want to be, imagine how awesome the world could become if we weren't limited by some external factor.

In the absence of a "meaningful dream" most people cannot "fix themselves" no matter what incentive they are offered.

Annie McKee *2011 ICF Philadelphia Coaches Conference*

As a young child, when asked what I wanted to be when I grew up, I had a standard answer. I want to be a part time ballet dancer and a part time trash truck driver.

Being a parent now, I can only imagine how my mother must have felt when I shared my thoughts! If my kids were to tell me that this was their dream, I believe that I would be thrilled, such creativity! But I'm certain many people would think this an odd career choice☺

Kids do say funny things. They have a pure innocence and clarity of purpose that we could all try to emulate and the world would be a better place. Clearly I was not trying to fit in at that point in my life.

Had I said it trying to get a laugh, that would have been one thing but I was dead serious. How did I find such a diverse answer to the age old question, "What do you want to be when you grow up?" I grew up playing trucks with my older brother; we were less than two years apart. The trash truck that actually "smashed" trash fascinated me - what a marvel of modern engineering. And to this day I continue to be amazed by the potential for technological advances - who thinks of these things? A big huge truck that all the trash goes in, and the power and control that the person pulling the handle possesses to be able to smash all the trash. But as exciting as driving a trash truck and pulling the handle to smash the trash was…I knew it wasn't enough to fill my soul. I also wanted to be a dancer on stage.

Again thinking of myself as a parent of a child who wanted two part time careers that were "rather diverse", would I have tried to convince them to make another plan?

Pick the one they liked more? Or the one that was more lucrative?

Or the one that had more job opportunities and room for growth?

My plan was to drive around and pick up the trash in the early AM, go to the studio and practice dance in the afternoon, and perform at night. It was my vision and I was too young and naïve to think it was strange or unusual. It's funny how art reflects our realities. Years later there was a film about a young woman who was a welder by day and dancer by night - Flashdance. I loved that movie, I so connected with the possibility of someone having more than one passion/career. This was similar to my original plan; who knew a movie could reflect my aspirations ?

Circling back to Annie's quote, remember that it's not the "incentives" or "stuff" that will make your life what you want it to be. You need to find your own personal "meaningful" dream. While my dream has changed and I no longer plan to be a professional dancer or trash truck driver, I have a new "meaningful" dream of my own. But what I learned is that many of us do not have just one passion or dream. There is room in our lives for many outlets whether as a career, hobby, recreation or as a volunteer. Don't give up on your dreams; they may become your future. What's your unique "meaningful" dream?

You might put on "What a Feeling" from Flashdance sung by Irene Cara to inspire your dreaming about what gives you that amazing feeling of reaching your own personal dream. If you don't already know, spend some time discovering what you yearn for this week!

"You may never have proof of your importance but you are more important than you think. There are always those who couldn't do without you. The rub is that you don't always know who." ~ Robert Fulghum, *All I Really Need to Know I Learned in Kindergarten*

Now that you have completed this Connection key skill section, do you feel like you have more clarity about how you can potentially navigate a career, college, or whatever option you choose beyond high school?

Have you:

- Discovered your Why?
- Completed your valuable research about your potential career paths?
- Learned about mentors and internships?
- Chosen a hero to inspire you?
- Reviewed potential alternatives to beyond high school paths?

If you cannot answer YES to all the questions above, go back and complete the unfinished exercises. If you can answer all these questions with a YES, you are ready to march forward to the Communication key skill for success section. Now that you have discovered your connections, you will learn to focus more clearly on communicating who you are. Keep putting yourself out there and taking advantage of any opportunities offered to gain experience and knowledge to define and develop your *Project of You Beyond High School Plan.*

COMMUNICATION

COMMUNICATION CAN BE defined as using words, signs, behaviors, or sounds to share or exchange information or ideas with someone else. While it sounds simplistic, it can be a complicated task to authentically share your exact meaning.

Communication is by far one of the most important skills you can develop for any Project of You Plan. For any field or industry you choose, being able to share your ideas and concerns is essential. You will need to be able to share both verbal and written ideas with others to be successful. Now that you have started making your connections, continuing to build your personal brand through positive communication is vital to reaching your future goals.

Consider a time in your life when you tried to communicate specific information with someone else and it was not easy. Communicating effectively takes practice.

In this key skill section you will:

- Learn the 2 golden rules for 1:1 communication
- Develop communication success skills
- Review the 13C's for positive communication
- Find Your Unique Voice
- Discover how to empower and advocate for yourself

After completing the readings and exercises in this section, you will have stronger communication skills; an investment in your future success for your entire life. Marching forward with your newly acquired skills will make it easier to complete your Project of You Plan beyond high school.

Two Golden rules for 1:1 communication success

My advice for any situation where you need to have a direct communication with another person involves two specific overall rules.

First, make sure you begin the conversation with a positive so that you begin in a place of positive energy rather than immediately causing that person to be on the defensive and raise their level of negative and victim energy. An example might be a scene you often see in romance movies. The person starts by saying "we need to talk" and given their intonation and inflection, the other person perceives there is a problem in the relationship.

How could that person have framed that statement differently to avoid putting the other person on the defensive? Often times using "I" statements avoids that defensive feeling. Imagine if the person said, *"I have something I wanted to share with you"* or *"I wanted to explain to you how I was feeling about..."* Now the person doesn't perceive an issue. Remember that you can't tell someone else what to do or how to feel, but you can always share how a situation makes you feel and that may or may not solve an issue for you.

Second, always think through what you want to say before you say it and consider how it would make you feel. This is called being compassionate. While in some cases, the message may not make the person feel good, your delivery and tone can make it easier for that person to hear. When you tell them what you think, consider their feelings and be aware that as long as you are honest and fair, you are not being a bad person. But again, don't use YOU; use "I" statements. Starting statements with "You" puts people on the defensive.

Develop Communication success skills

Your personal communication style is a skill that you develop throughout your life and is a refection of the unique individual that you choose to project to the outside world. Communication is about more than just exchanging information, or writing or saying words.

There are several communication success skills that are worth practicing and perfecting. Whenever possible, before speaking or writing to someone, consider these three important themes.

1. Always consider the receiver of your message:

   Know your audience and do your research before a meeting request. Never go into a meeting without research and preparation; you can find out the basics about almost anyone or anything online now.

   Think about how your receiver feels before you speak. Try to tune into your intuition and non-verbal cues before responding; always consider your receiver's feelings.

   Consider the receiver's perspective and goals; you have your agenda for the discussion or meeting and the person(s) you are meeting with do as well. Set expectations for the goals and timeframe at the beginning of the discussion or meeting. Have your agenda and goals in writing whenever possible to maintain focus.

2. Know your intended outcome and craft your message with that goal in mind:

   How do you project yourself but make it about WIIFT (What's in it for them): If you are asking someone to do an internship at their company, be prepared to tell them why it's to their advantage to work with you. What can you do to help them? It's not simply that you want to gain experience or someone recommended it.

   How to ask for what you want, first by knowing what you want:

start off your discussion or meeting being clear about why you requested their valuable time and what you want to accomplish.

Stop and focus before responding: what do you want? What do they want? You are in a meeting with a college admission's representative. You want them to accept you into their program. They want to choose the most qualified candidates. Stay focused on showing them your motivation and your amazing skills and accomplishments so they want to make you an offer.

3. Preparation through practice

Practice and Role Play before important events: write out possible scenarios for an admissions interview, job interview, informational interview, debate or other important event. Practice delivering your message by role-playing with your accountability partner or another trusted advisor.

Make eye contact: never avoid eye contact with your receiver; making eye contact shows you are confident and creates a stronger connection.

Consider your tone: you need to learn that everything you say or write also conveys your feelings and intentions. You want the receiver to hear or read your message, exactly the way you intended. This is not a simple task but with practice you can perfect it. Think about a time when your message was taken incorrectly and how you could have improved that communication.

Non- verbal cues: learning to notice non-verbal cues such as gestures, posture, eye rolling, distracted unengaged listening, and facial expressions will help you to communicate better and understand how your message is being received. Watch others non-verbal cues and learn from them and also consider your non-verbal cues whenever possible.

Verbal Pace: do you speak too fast or too slowly? If anyone has ever told you that you speak too fast or too slowly, take this as constructive criticism and practice and role-play improving your verbal pace.

WAIT rule: why am I talking? Every moment does not need to be filled with conversation. There are times when a pause can be very powerful. In some cases, you need to give your receiver time to process and consider what you have just said. Practice and role-play being comfortable with pauses.

Active listening: it is a very important skill to actively listen and digest what your receiver is saying also. Many people are so busy thinking about what they want to say next that they don't process what is being said.

This is an important skill in any profession but consider these two examples.

A doctor who is trying to diagnose an illness needs to listen carefully to all your symptoms and then ask more questions to be certain they provide you the right treatment.

A salesperson has a product they are trying to sell, it may be more expensive than the customer's budget. But if the salesperson truly understands the customer's pain and can explain how the product can solve their pain, the customer might be willing to spend the extra money.

Perfecting your communication skills helps you deepen your connections to others and improve teamwork, decision-making, and problem solving. It enables you to communicate even negative or difficult messages without creating conflict or destroying trust. You can improve your communication skills through practice but remember to be authentic and your message will be more effective.

More than just the words you use, effective communication combines a set of skills including nonverbal communication, attentive listening, managing stress in the moment, the ability to communicate assertively, and the capacity to recognize and understand your own emotions and those of the person you're communicating with.

Of course, it takes time and effort to develop these skills and become an effective communicator. The more effort and practice you put in, the more instinctive and spontaneous your communication skills will become.

Download your **Communication Assessment Worksheet** from my website: www.marchforwardconsulting.com or utilize **the Communication Assessment Worksheet** in **The Project of You Workbook**.

What do you need to work on?

The 13 C's of communication beyond high school

As you venture on beyond high school into college, a career, technical school or GAP year, it is assumed that you have mastered communication. In my work with young adults fairly new to the workplace in internships and new jobs, I receive many questions about how to potentially handle various "somewhat complicated and unclear" situations. Given the variety of questions and situations, I am sharing overarching communication key skills for success to practice and utilize as you feel comfortable. While communication techniques and styles can be extremely personal, learning the important basic key skills for success is crucial.

Some of the key skills for success give examples of workplace situations but they can be universally applied to situations in high school relationships, college team projects, and any other collaborative situations working with others to accomplish a goal.

As technology such as email, text, twitter, FB, etc. have changed potential communication in the workplace, carefully considering your personal delivery style and content and what you share becomes an even bigger issue. Understanding how technology works and the fact that written texts and emails do not have the inflections and gestures that verbal speech provides, they can be misinterpreted.

When you are speaking to someone directly, you can determine their reaction to your statements through facial expressions and gestures, and you have the opportunity to clarify but this is not the case in written communications.

Remember anything that you type or post is accessible in the future. It is permanent in some format, online, in your cell phone records, in another person's cell phone records, in an email or on your laptop or tablet. Technology experts can trace anything you type or record back to you, so don't document anything you wouldn't be comfortable with having someone else read in the future.

While you learn to talk and communicate somewhat "naturally" as children, you learn words, as you need them, to describe what you want and how to ask for it.

You like bananas and learn the word "bananas", and that your Mom expects you add the word "please" at the end of any request. Pretty simple. This is an age-old process, and works perfectly well for young people who follow the standards as part of a family or within their education system.

But it can be difficult adapting to a new culture in a college or career setting. In addition, technology has changed our communication styles considerably, and the standards for communications via various technology modalities are not 100% clear and consistent in any industry. I have not specifically addressed technology such as email templates and standards in this book. That is a large topic and needs to be addressed but there's enough information for it to be a separate book. This book covers general guidelines for communication and developing your personal communication style as an adult. Your communication style as an adult in the working world is generally significantly evolved from that of your younger self.

Throughout your life, you make shifts in who you are - change is a constant.

In a commencement speech at West Chester University, Dr. Oz shared,

"We need to be aware that the average relationship lasts only 7 years unless you re-invent it.

He explained that "he has been married to his lovely wife Lisa for 26 years so he has actually been married to 4 different women".

As you re-invent every 7 years, you may want to re-invent your communication style both in personal and business relationships.

You can understand how important strong communication skills are when you review the impact communication has on whether or not people remain in their jobs. Here are ten critical reasons why employees quit their job. Items # 1-7 are all within your personal control but will require strong, effective communication skills to potentially resolve if they arise.

1. Relationship with boss

2. Bored and unchallenged by the work itself

3. Relationships with co-workers

4. Opportunities to use skills and abilities

5. Contribution of work to the organization's business goals

6. Autonomy and independence

7. Meaningfulness of job

8. Organization's financial stability

9. Overall corporate culture

10. Management's recognition of employee job performance

The types of issues in items # 1 – 7 are within your control if you learn how to ask for what you want in a positive, productive way.

You can see how important developing strong, effective

communication skills is to having a happy, healthy, fulfilling career path to maintain your self-supporting status.

Communication starts with the letter C and so do the 13 characteristics I've listed below. This is a very "high-level, beginning to scratch the surface" document on the subject of professional communications to give you some things to think about as you transition from high school to college or technical school or an internship or a career. While reading and doing the exercises, consider how you want make a shift in the way you utilize "your unique voice and your personal brand".

Starting a new job, heading off to college, or becoming certified at a technical school can be a big challenge due to nervousness and uncertainty, the stress and anxiety that typically goes along with any new situation in your life. While your high school may have been a more informal setting, your new future setting may feel somewhat overwhelming given the differing environment and culture. Many companies have started having a more casual environment in terms of dress codes and flexible hours, but it is important to know yourself and set your boundaries for success by presenting yourself professionally both as far as dress and most importantly in terms of your communication with others.

Establishing yourself as a clear communicator by demonstrating the13C Communication Characteristics will be crucial for success.

If you are:

1. confident,
2. constructive,
3. cheerful,
4. concise,
5. clarifying,
6. candid,
7. considerate,
8. consistent,

9. coachable

10. compassionate,

11. complimentary,

12. connect with others, and

13. choose your words carefully,

you are certain to find success. Be sure that you know the meaning of each of these and how it would be useful in a school or work setting. More detailed information about each characteristic is provided. It is never too early to start preparing for your future and adopting good communication habits.

1. Confident:

Being confident in your own ideas as you speak will shine through with every word. If you doubt yourself and don't believe in yourself, others will doubt you too.

This is important both with your friends as well as with the influencers in your life.

Confidence in a discussion also means being able to admit when you do not know something. In any situation, never leave another person wondering what to expect moving forward. It is also important to be confident with others to both show what you know, as well as be willing to ask questions as needed. No reasonable teacher or employer expects you to know everything. But they do want someone confident enough to ask when they are unclear about what to do next or how to complete a specific task. Remember what your teachers and professors have told you for years - there is no such thing as a stupid question, and this is true.

Believe in yourself and others will believe in you!

~ Brenda Jo March

In many cases, preparation is key to being confident, so always **"Be Prepared"**. There's a reason it's the Boy Scouts motto.

2. Constructive:

Learning to offer constructive comments whether to a co-worker, friend, family member, or anyone else in your life is a very important and often delicate skill to develop. If you have a concern, make certain that you present it as a constructive concern about the work you are doing, not about a specific person or personal issue.

Remember that accomplishing a task is about:

- making something happen,
- solving a problem,
- and many other tasks,

but it is not personal.

Learning to deliver your messages constructively is a gift that will assist you in all areas of your life and in every relationship.

"A true artist removes his heart willingly, allows constructive criticism to stomp it, then puts it back—bruised and aching—as he continues to strive for excellence due to the all-consuming obsession and love for his art."
~ H.G. Mewis

3. Cheerful:

Like constructive, cheerful is a general rule of communication in any situation. No one wants to be with or work with people who are negative. Cheerful has more to do with how you deliver the message than your actual message content.

Being able to deliver a message with a pleasant demeanor does not always come naturally to everyone, so it may require some effort on your part if it is not your natural tendency. Consider the people you know who have a cheerful demeanor and typically cheerful delivery. Is it more pleasant to collaborate with them on projects than the "grouches"?

Learning to control your mind, your lizard brain, "Amygdala" when you are angry or frustrated is very important to being able to maintain a cheerful attitude.

If you have trouble controlling your angry impulses, it may be worthwhile to consider a stress management or anger management class so that you can develop skills to discourage your "Amygdala" from taking control. The more you are able to manage your stress and anger, the more you will be able to be cheerful with your co-workers.

Consider how often you become angry and frustrated. Do you need some assistance with learning to be more cheerful? If yes, there are many programs online and live workshops available; enroll in one.

> *"Cheerfulness and contentment are great beautifiers and are famous preservers of youthful looks."*
>
> *~ Charles Dickens*

4. Concise:

Concise is giving a lot of information clearly and in a few words; brief but comprehensive. Learning to be impeccable and concise with your message is key to being valued as a contributor. Don't feel the need to speak just because you are participating. If you have new information, valuable insights or ideas definitely share them but be clear and concise during your message.

> *"I love songs because by nature they are concise; they sum up. I try to use as few words as possible. It's usually funnier that way, anyway."*
>
> *~ Cass McCombs*

5. Clarifying:

Clarifying what is expected of you is extremely important in any situation.

Do not flounder and be unclear and do not assume; we all know what assuming means.

In some cases, clarifying may mean defining a term. Some definitions are open to interpretation and not concrete.

Your definition of flexible and your supervisor's can be extremely different.

You may assume that you are able to arrive at 10am, take a 3-hour lunch daily, and leave at 4pm as long as your work is completed.

Her idea of flexible may have been that you can arrive at 9:15 instead of 8:30 once or twice a month without it being an issue.

Clearly these two definitions of flexibility are very different and need to be clarified.

It is very important to clarify all aspects of a working relationship before starting the position. You must all continue to clarify potential differences in vision as they arise. Having and maintaining clarity in any potential project and/or relationship is the only way to be certain that you are all "on the same page" and avoid conflicts.

> *"When you assume, you make an ass out of u and me."*
> *~ Oscar Wilde*

> *"Words are powerful. When I make mistakes I just try to come back and clarify what I meant."*
> *~ Soulja Boy*

6. Candid:

The definition of candid is: openly straightforward and direct without reserve or secretiveness. If you're too candid in your personal social media, a future employer might discover something about you that is not impressive.

Being open and honest is generally always the best policy but this does not mean that you need to tell everyone every personal detail of your life.

As you grew up, you learned to develop a filter for your personal life. You may have a best friend that you tell everything but only after years of building that relationship and the trust that has grown with it. Perhaps you have other close friends that you share a lot with, but not as much as your best friend. Then you may have teachers, parents, grandparents or other adults with whom you may only share limited filtered details of your personal life. This level of filtering is best in any new relationships.

Another person's values may not match yours exactly. Try to think back to a time in middle school when you shared too much with an inconsiderate person; remember how that turned out. Perhaps a confidence was broken, or a bully made something personal about you public, or a statement was taken out of context and you or someone else were hurt? Even in the adult world there are people who are not respectful of others' feelings and privacy. As the saying goes, "always err on the side of caution".

"People are afraid because I'm candid. They're always worried I'm going to get into trouble."

~ Steve Madden

7. Connecting:

Make the most of any opportunities to connect with others about topics that aren't generally so personal. Always make an effort to ask the other person questions about themselves first. If you find an area of common interest, explore that and remember that connection. Perhaps you have both traveled to Tahiti and thought it was the most beautiful place in the world. Sharing your preferences around things like music, movies, travel, fitness, food, fashion and other leisure activities are generally ways to make a connection to others, without potential conflict.

These connections will help others truly remember you; we meet so many people daily in our fast paced world. As is often quoted, don't bring up politics or religion with people you don't know well. These tend to be very personal subjects. Sometimes others are offended by your viewpoint.

Have a "go to" question ready to use when you feel uncomfortable and want to change subjects or a reason to excuse yourself. Perhaps something like: "Forgive me for changing topics but I've always wanted to ask you what originally brought you to this company?" Or something else specific to that person, that might be a connecting point between the two of you. "I haven't had a minute to ask but I know you are an avid skier and my friends are planning a trip to Park City, Utah. Have you ever skied there?"

Creating, building, and maintaining relationships are arguably the most important skills you can develop. "No man is an island"; we all need to connect and live and work together in some form. If you feel like you have trouble connecting with others, seek some assistance with this skill. There are workshops, books, courses and coaches and mentors ready to assist you to improve your ability to connect to others and build and maintain relationships.

The actual skill of connecting with other people can be taught, practiced and honed. For some it may come more naturally than to others but that does not mean that it cannot be learned. The long-term value to you, of being able to make stronger, more meaningful, lasting connections will be worth the effort to learn this skill.

"I define connection as the energy that exists between people when they feel seen, heard, and valued; when they can give and receive without judgment; and when they derive sustenance and strength from the relationship."

~ Brene Brown

8. Considerate

The definition of considerate is: thinking about the rights and feelings of other people, or showing kindness toward other people.

It is important in any setting - class, face-to-face meeting, or phone call - to be respectful of others' feelings, ideas, and opinions. Everyone deserves an opportunity to offer their thoughts and ideas and receive feedback so that they can learn and grow.

Everyone wants to be heard and valued. If you are running a meeting, look around and ask those who haven't spoken if they have anything they want to add. Use your intuition. At times, you may see a person who looks like they have something to add but you know they aren't the type to speak up. In this moment, find a way to offer them the floor. This can be difficult to orchestrate but get in the habit of asking each participant if they want to add anything at the end of the event.

In social situations outside of work activities, being considerate of others regarding your topics and trying to include everyone that is in your small area will show your kind nature and professionalism. It will also help you to increase your connection and show your natural leadership abilities. If you don't typically think of others, start now; it's an important quality for success.

"Really big people are, above everything else, courteous, considerate and generous - not just to some people in some circumstances - but to everyone all the time."
~ Thomas J. Watson

Bonus: Do you know who Thomas J. Watson is?

9. Consistent:

A great leader is a consistent performer and communicator.

When others know you are dependable both at getting your work done or leading a team and in providing consistent information, they will enjoy working with you!

If you are someone whose communication and behavior is dictated by mood swings and people don't know what they can expect - "The Jekyll and Hide" syndrome - this does not create a pleasant environment.

I'm sure you have all experienced a friend, teacher or coach who took out their frustrations in the classroom or on the practice field by yelling, being rude, and adding negative energy that made life very uncomfortable.

With people who haven't learned to be consistent, every situation is unpredictable. They are also often impulsive, basically the opposite of consistent. An occasional unique pleasant surprise is a good thing but an unpleasant surprise from an inconsistent performer is very frustrating. It's hard to trust someone if you don't know what they might say or how they are going to behave in a given situation. Being consistent becomes more natural as you increase your self-awareness, knowing yourself, and identifying situations that stress you. How to positively cope in tough situations will allow you to become more consistent. As you continue to get to know yourself, you will be able to be more consistent because you will also be more authentic.

Remember that being consistent can also be a bad thing if you consistently procrastinate, miss deadlines, act impulsively, respond negatively or see the bad side of any situation. This is a consistent pattern but not one for success.

You want to consistently provide a clear, concise, and confident message about who you are and what can be expected from you as a participant or a leader.

> *"The secret to winning is constant, consistent management."*
>
> *~ Tom Landry*

10. Coachable:

Being open to others' ideas and questions and willing to take direction as needed is being coachable. No one wants to work with a person <u>unwilling</u> to consider a different point of view or not open to learning, change, and growth. Almost all experienced, successful business leaders, athletes, and entertainers have someone coaching them.

They may be receiving coaching on:

- what to say,
- how to perform,
- how to handle a difficult situation,
- better decision making,
- helping them develop long term goals and
- being their accountability partner.

These are just a few of the ways that a coach/mentor may assist another to grow.

The only constant in our world is change. And every experience is an opportunity for growth. Every person we meet is both our teacher and our student so enjoy the experiences that you are provided. Listen, consider the feedback, and try doing things differently. If you get the outcome or feedback that you desire with the new process, being coachable was an asset to you. Allow yourself to be coachable.

Coachability is the willingness to be corrected and to act on that correction. When we are coachable, we are prepared to be wrong. Many people being coached hold tightly to their own personal limiting beliefs or assumptions of why something is not possible. If you are not open to new possibilities, you are not coachable. No one is always right and learning is a lifelong process so enjoy it! Being coachable is not an easy task. We are taught to be independent and think for ourselves, and we form habits based on our ideas. People that are completely coachable are very rare but also generally the most successful. Try it!

"Failure is good. It's fertilizer. Everything I've learned about coaching, I've learned from making mistakes."

~ Rick Pitino

11. Compassionate:

Compassion literally means, "to suffer together." Among emotional researchers, it is defined as the feeling that arises when you are confronted with another's suffering and you feel motivated to relieve that suffering.

Compassion is not the same as empathy. Empathy refers more generally to our ability to take the perspective of and feel the emotions of another person; compassion is when those feelings and thoughts include the desire to help. We all have good days and bad days. It's thus important to be compassionate and consider how another person might feel. Always think about how you feel when you are in the same position. Try to use your intuition and consider the other person's circumstances.

If you are truly compassionate in your thoughts and words, others will feel it and respect you and appreciate it. We are all here to support each other so before speaking, consider how the person receiving your message may feel. In some cases you may have to deliver a tough message but it can be delivered in a compassionate way. If you have to deliver negative feedback, always offer some positive feedback as an opening statement.

Your mother may have taught you that if you don't have anything nice to say, don't say anything at all. While that is not a bad rule of thumb, it may be necessary to share something not nice occasionally. In those moments, start with a positive affirmation and be compassionate.

"The purpose of human life is to serve, and to show compassion and the will to help others. "
~ Albert Schweitzer

12. Complimentary:

Whenever possible be complimentary to others. This creates positive energy and strengthens relationships and synergy within your group.

Be authentic in your compliments. Don't just make things up to "brown nose" but don't be afraid to share. If someone does a great job on a project, tell him or her about it - don't hesitate! Each time you thank someone for doing something that matters to you, they will likely do it again. When someone has a new haircut or some other change that you truly think is a good change, tell him or her about it. Many times when you pay someone a compliment, it generates additional discussion and allows for deepening of the relationship. Use any opportunities to show how observant and caring you can be naturally, by being a complimentary person.

"Sincere compliments cost nothing and can accomplish so much. In ANY relationship, they are the applause that refreshes."
~ Steve Goodier

13. Choice:

Choice consists of a mental decision, of judging the merits of multiple options and selecting one or more of them.

So all of your communications are a choice:

- to speak or not to speak,
- to respond or not respond to an email or text,
- how you deliver your message, the content, the style, the format,
- and the feeling of your words are all purely up to you - your choice.

You are the only one in control of how your unique, individual communications affect the course of your life and the lives of the people receiving your communications.

It is your choice to be in any interaction and to be a cheerful, positive communicator.

If you make the correct choices, you will be successful.

Your communications are the only way you reflect your choices; think about that!

Also consider that increasing your self-awareness will allow you more choices. You can't change or make choices without knowing who you truly are at your core being.

"We all make choices, but in the end our choices make us."

~ Ken Levine

Download your **Communication 13C's Worksheet** from my website: www.marchforwardconsulting.com or utilize the **Communication 13C's Worksheet** in The Project of You Workbook.

After reviewing the 13C's for communication success, pick three words that you feel are the key skills for success you need to master for the most improvement. Write them down and write examples of when this concept has been a struggle for you or why you have chosen this concept.

Review your list with your accountability partner and develop a SMART goal of how you will work on this concept over the next 3 months.

Perhaps if you feel that clarifying is something you need to work on, you can create a standard line that you use to clarify with another person such as, " To be sure I understand, can I repeat back to you what I just heard?"

If you use that statement at least twice a week for three months, it will become a habit for you and allow you to be more comfortable clarifying with others. You may not be comfortable asking for clarification or you may feel it shows a weakness but this is not true. It is important to not walk away unclear in any setting whether a learning environment or a work setting. How can you digest what you heard or move ahead with a project or request if you aren't clear

regarding exactly what was being taught or what was asked of you.

Remember, there is no such thing as a stupid question. Better to ask

now then send an email or text hours or days later. It saves you time and

gives the person you are interacting with assurance that you are engaged.

"Chica, if you ask a question it makes you look stupid for 5

minutes – but if you don't ask – you stay stupid for fifty years, so

always ask questions in your life."

http://www.experienceproject.com/question-answer/A-Teacher-

Once-Said-There-Is-No-Such-Thing-As-A-Stupid-Question-Is-She-

Right-Or-Wrong/1801871

FIND YOUR UNIQUE VOICE

FINDING YOUR UNIQUE voice will allow you to confidently share your ideas. Throughout your life you will continue to improve your communication and leadership skills. To be successful in life, you need to be empowered for whatever mission you choose. In addition, you need to be able to effectively communicate your thoughts and ideas both to individuals and groups.

My goals for you are:

- To increase your self-awareness & self confidence
- To develop your unique voice
- To learn to release your fears around sharing your unique voice
- To learn active listening
- To encourage others and provide constructive feedback
- To practice organizing and presenting your unique ideas

In the book *Outliers*, author Malcolm Gladwell says that it takes roughly ten thousand hours of practice to achieve mastery in a field. Decide how you can work on your first few hours needed to get you started on the path towards your ten thousand hours in pursuit of becoming a confident speaker and communicator.

While many of you may not be interested in pursuing a career in public speaking, it is a skill that will serve you well regardless of the profession that you choose to pursue.

As you move ahead in your life, there may also be causes that you may want to advocate for, or social issues that you would like to become a part of changing. Your ability to share your unique voice and amazing ideas will serve you well in those efforts.

Download the **TED – like talk Worksheet** from my website: www.marchforwardconsulting.com or utilize the **TED – like talk Worksheet** in The Project of You Workbook.

Pick one of your career ideas and develop a "TED" like talk between two to eight minutes describing what you have learned and why you are passionate about this potential career. Share this talk with your mentor or accountability partner or offer to deliver it to a class for their enhancement. Practice the delivery of your speech and be sure not to just read your words. If your speech appears spontaneous and authentic, it will have a greater impact.

EMPOWER AND ADVOCATE FOR YOU

EMPOWERMENT IS DEFINED as being given power or authority. As you march forward in your life, you will give yourself more power and authority to make your own choices. And advocate is defined as to speak, write or stand up for something or someone.

Be able to advocate for yourself, ask for help or walk away if that is best for you. While it may not always be comfortable, giving yourself permission to be empowered will change your world for the better. I have met strong, independent, academically and socially successful young adults who have felt overwhelmed and found no where to turn when authority does not listen or care about what they have to say.

One such example is Grace. *I met a young woman Grace who was a successful student athlete and very confident but a true "people pleaser". She was smart, capable, compassionate, and appeared self -confident. According to her parents, she was also stubborn and strong willed and often challenged them. Grace's parents never worried about her at school. She was well established at her school as responsible and involved. Grace was cooperative, caring, excited about school activities and loved all that came with the social aspects of her school. Gym was her favorite subject and her gym teacher was her favorite teacher.*

One evening Grace hurt her foot during a soccer game. She did not see a doctor, as it was late. The next day Grace was still in significant pain but she felt that she would be ok at school. In the morning rush, neither

169

Grace nor her parents thought about her having gym that day and writing a note to be excused though her foot was visibly swollen and bruised. For those of you who are athletic, perhaps you can relate, as injuries are just a part of the process.

When Grace got to gym class that day, she explained to her "favorite" teacher what had happened. The teacher required her to run on it, even though she told him that she was injured and in significant pain, because she didn't have a note. She did what she was told without question and not feeling empowered, kept trying to be a people pleaser even as it caused her physical pain. When Grace did get to the doctor later that day, she had a hairline fracture. Grace should not have run on an injured foot but she didn't feel she had a choice.

What could Grace have done differently if she felt empowered?

Talking to Grace later, I asked why she didn't ask to go to the nurse, or the principal, or explain that she was simply in too much pain to run. She said it didn't cross her mind to not do as she was told. And while the physical pain was severe, she felt emotional pain too. Grace needed permission to be empowered and know that if it caused her true physical or emotional pain, she could refuse or walk away.

Grace was so hurt and insulted that her favorite teacher didn't believe her. Grace's parents explained to her that if a similar situation ever occurred again, she had their permission to walk out and find another adult such as another teacher, the school nurse, the principal, or anyone who would listen to what she felt and had to say. While this was a painful lesson for Grace, it generated much learning and positive discussion to prepare Grace for being on her own.

Intuition, judgment, compassion, and caring should come into play in a situation like this one, not simply policy and procedure. Many wonderful teachers are trying to comply with the many rules and standards that they are expected to follow. It's not an easy job and we are all only human and have our bad days. Learning to be empowered and advocate for you is a valuable lesson.

The key here is that you need to find your ability to empower yourself when there are difficult choices and you need to advocate for yourself!

No one is going to come to you and hold your hand or walk you through the process of planning your life - even on a smaller scale, as just deciding what to do next, beyond high school. There are so many choices and it's hard for anyone to sift through all the information available now.

One of the most important things you can develop as a student is the ability to advocate for yourself. In many cases as a student, your parents and guardians would do the advocating for you. If there was a problem with a teacher or a bully or a health issue or any other concern, your parents and guardians handled the situation and facilitated the necessary discussions. Many students have not learned to speak up or advocate for themselves because they have strong proactive parents and guardians who believe they are doing the best for their children.

This is a skill that will serve you well in any situation, whether college or in the working world; advocating for what you need is empowering. This of course assumes that you know what you need as we discussed earlier.

Never be afraid to ask for help and don't wait for someone to ask you what you need.

This may be a new skill for you in college, as you are on your own for the first time, but never be afraid to ask for help.

Download the **Empower Me Worksheet** from my website: www. marchforwardconsulting.com or utilize the **Empower Me Worksheet** in **The Project of You Workbook.**

Share and discuss with your group or accountability partner or trusted advisor.

ALWAYS PREPARE FOR AN INTERVIEW

AN INTERVIEW IS a formal meeting where you are being assessed for your qualifications or asked questions to give an expert opinion. Some examples include: a college admissions interview, a job applicant interview, or a radio talk show interview. As you march forward completing your *Project of You Plan* beyond high school, there are many times that you may have to go on an interview. You may have already been on a job interview or been interviewed for an article in the school newspaper. Colleges and technical schools may require interviews or you may be interviewed to make a decision on a scholarship award. Whatever the reason, it is important to be prepared for your upcoming interviews. Spend some time considering what you might be asked and how you will answer. For additional preparation, there are numerous online sites with interview questions, skills, and tips.

I have included my 10 most important interview tips worksheet for you to read and complete. I also highly recommend that you practice role-play interviewing with your group or accountability partner or trusted advisor. Before any interview or important meeting, complete or review this list to be prepared. This list was written for job seekers, but can be adapted if you are using it for college interviews.

The 10 Most Important Interview Tips

1. Be Prepared

    a. Research the company/college – what do you need to know?

    b. Research the position/majors

    c. Research the salary/extracurricular activities

    d. Have questions ready - what is your "go to" question?

    e. Talk to other employees/students & professors

    f. Know the Culture/Core Values

    g. Be ready to explain: Why YOU want to work/attend school there?

    h. Arrive a few minutes early: consider traffic & parking

2. NO cell phone during the meeting – turn it off and put it away!

3. Establish Rapport ASAP

    a. The first 30 seconds are the most important

    b. Make eye contact

    c. Ask an open ended positive question – one that cannot be answered with yes or no.

    d. Find a common ground/point of connection

4. Be Natural: Be yourself – it's mutually beneficial to present the real you

5. Don't Appear Desperate

6. Use appropriate language

7. Listen & answer questions

    a. Have examples of your experience on the tip of your tongue.

    b. Review most common interview questions and have answers prepped

8. Three C's – Cool, calm, confident - not cocky

9. Be confident discussing compensation/admission & next steps

10. The interview is not the time for negotiating but do share any special requirements so not perceived as a bait and switch

Write your answers and thoughts out & practice!

Putting your intentions into writing gives them a life of their own, even if it's on a napkin!

~ Brenda Jo March

Remember: **If your ship doesn't come in, you have to swim out to meet it.**

Now that you have completed this Communication Concept section, do you feel like you have more clarity about how you can potentially negotiate your path towards a career, college, or whatever option you choose beyond high school?

Have you:

1. Learned the 2 golden rules for 1:1 communication?

2. Developed and practiced communication success skills?

3. Reviewed the 13C's for positive communication?

4. Found Your Unique Voice?

5. Discovered how to empower and advocate for yourself?

6. Completed and role -played answers to your Interview questions?

If you cannot answer YES to all the questions above, go back and complete the unfinished exercises.

If you can answer all these questions with a YES, you are ready to march forward to the Values key skill for success section. You will learn to connect to your individual core values and how that affects your development of your Project of You Beyond High School Plan.

VALUES

"Your beliefs become your thoughts, Your thoughts become your words, Your words become your actions, Your actions become your habits, Your habits become your values, and Your values become your destiny."

~ Mahatma Gandhi

NOW THAT YOU'VE taken the time to learn to budget your time and set goals, discover who you are and what you want, made your connections, researched your options, and worked on your communication skills, it's time to get clear on your core values.

In this concept section you will:

1. Learn about the concept of core values

2. Develop Your Core Values

3. Research institution and organizational core values

4. Get real with $

5. Consider your passions

6. Decide how you will help others

After completing the readings and exercises in this section, you will have a stronger understanding of your individual core values and how you fit into the world beyond high school. Understanding your

values will make it easier to complete your *Project of You Plan* and

march forward beyond high school. This clarity will help you learn

to research and choose institutions to attend and organizations to

become involved with that match your personal core values.

UNCOVER YOUR CORE VALUES?

What are Core Values? Your personal core values are one-word statements that connect your heart and mind and help to define your real self. The term "core values" is used often by coaches and counselors but has also become a way for institutions and organizations to provide insight into their unique culture and beliefs. Only you will able to determine which core values are most critical to your health, happiness and life satisfaction.

Some examples of core values include:

Justice	Freedom	Safety
Family	Integrity	Accomplishments
Ethical	Dependable	Forgiving
Compassionate		Honest

This list of positive core values may be some that you feel define your priorities.

Not all core values are positive. If you are self centered or greedy, these are core values that will drive your behaviors and your decisions. What motivates and drives your life is your choice. There are no "right" or "wrong" values for you. If you acknowledge and live by your core values, your actions will "feel good". If you don't accept and live by your core values, you will feel "bad" and not in balance.

In many cases, adults who have not established clear work/life balance will feel stressed and unhappy because they are not living by their core values. As an example, if one of their primary core values is "family comes first", but work is taking priority, life is not good. In this case, a person would need to learn to establish positive boundaries at work to allow for family time. Seeking assistance to be accountable for knowing and living your values helps these people feel good again.

Your core values direct how you use your time and energy. If you have devoted large amounts of your time and energy to something based on what someone else wants you to do and it doesn't align with your core values, you will not be satisfied with your life path.

Without recognizing your most important core values, you may be less driven to achieve your goals, seeking something that makes you feel "right" about your path. Recognizing your core values will allow you to march forward toward your goals. By living your core values, you will feel positive and focused. People who live by their core values are able to more easily set and reach goals and are more content with their daily lives.

Download the **Core Values Worksheet** from my website: www.marchforwardconsulting.com or utilize the **Core Values Worksheet** in **The Project of You Workbook.**

CONNECTING TO OTHERS WITH SIMILAR CORE VALUES

Now that you have acknowledged your personal core values, how do you use this information to make decisions about your *Project of You Plan* for marching forward beyond high school? You will discover as you research your potential options that many post secondary schools and many organizations have defined their unique core values. Why? Defining core values helps organizations give potential connectors insight into their culture and also keeps them focused to fulfill their goals. Core values create a guide for students, employees, and clients. This is a key to success because connecting people with similar core values creates a stronger team. It also provides a guide for students, employees, and clients about what to expect if you choose to engage with a specific institution or organization.

You can research the core values statements of most institutions and organizations online. As an example of an institution, I have attached Penn State University's Core Values.

From PSU.edu:

The Penn State Values, a statement of core values for the University, was developed over a four-year process. The Values represent our core ethical aspirations for all our daily activities and actions as students, faculty, staff, and volunteers at Penn State.

The Values are as follows. Click on each for examples of the Values in action.

INTEGRITY: We act with integrity and honesty in accordance with the highest academic, professional, and ethical standards.

RESPECT: We respect and honor the dignity of each person, embrace civil discourse, and foster a diverse and inclusive community.

RESPONSIBILITY: We act responsibly, and we are accountable for our decisions, actions, and their consequences.

DISCOVERY: We seek and create new knowledge and understanding, and foster creativity and innovation, for the benefit of our communities, society, and the environment.

EXCELLENCE: We strive for excellence in all our endeavors as individuals, an institution, and a leader in higher education.

COMMUNITY: We work together for the betterment of our University, the communities we serve, and the world.

Knowing many students who attended PSU, I believe that their core values ring true. As a very large institution, the community they have built is amazing. I have seen first hand the power of the PSU community and network. I have also experienced first hand their core values such as responsibility, excellence, and discovery via PSU students I have met sharing their experiences about attending PSU.

You can research the core values of any institution you are planning to attend. If they are not visible on the institution's website, you can always use this as an interview question or in an individual email inquiry to learn more. Understanding the institution's core values may help you decide if it's a fit for you.

As an example of organizational core values that may affect your career choices, I have shared three very different organizations' core values. These three examples provide a snapshot of clear, interesting core values. I chose these examples because I know from personal experience and speaking with employees that they do embrace their core values daily at Urban Outfitters, Zappos and Ritz Carlton.

Knowing many employees at Urban Outfitters, I have learned a lot about their culture and core values. If you look at their website, you will learn even more. They have many benefits for their employees such as a bike program, fitness classes, onsite cafeteria, and many other bonuses. I believe the most unique fact about Urban Outfitters is the ability to bring your dog with you to work. This is taken from their website:

We make no bones about our devotion to canines. In almost every building at our Navy Yard campus, you can spot a furry fellow. Not only can employees bring their dogs to work, but they can also take them to our dog park for a quick break, enter them in our annual Halloween pup costume contest and receive pet insurance discounts. Let's just say man and woman's best friend are a welcomed addition to our employee base.

If you have a dog or wish you had a dog, this might be a great benefit for you. But the main reason I share this is because after learning more, you realize this is not your typical "corporate" culture.

Zappos Core Values:

As we grow as a company, it has become more and more important to explicitly define the core values from which we develop our culture, our brand, and our business strategies. These are the ten core values that we live by:

1. *Deliver WOW Through Service*

2. *Embrace and Drive Change*

3. *Create Fun and A Little Weirdness*

4. *Be Adventurous, Creative, and Open-Minded*

5. *Pursue Growth and Learning*

6. *Build Open and Honest Relationships With Communication*

7. *Build a Positive Team and Family Spirit*

8. *Do More With Less*

9. *Be Passionate and Determined*

10. *Be Humble*

As a pleased Zappos customer, I enjoyed learning more about their core values. In my interactions, I have known them to deliver WOW through service. In receiving shoes that didn't fit, they sent the new size before I returned the first pair. I have never had this happen with any other online store. I think the rest of their core values are self -explanatory and would be engaging to many potential employees. Their third value, "create fun and a little weirdness" gives you the sense of Zappos wanting to add humor and embrace differences in their organization. If you would like to be a part of a conventional, highly structured, typical corporate organization, then perhaps Zappos would not be a good fit for you. But if you are seeking an unconventional, unique culture, this may be the perfect company for you.

You can research the core values of any organization that you would potentially like to work for to learn more about the organization. If the core values are not readily visible on the organization's website, you can always use this as an interview question or in an individual email inquiry to learn more. Understanding the organization's core values may help you decide if it's a fit for you.

As another example, I've shared hotel chain Ritz Carlton's core values below.

Before each employee shift at the Ritz Carlton, the team reviews their 11 core values. This ensures that the employees are reminded of the environment Ritz Carlton is trying to create. Imagine being inspired and motivated by values such as these in your future career. Do these core values match your core values and resonate with you?

1. *Foster close relationships with guests so they always stay at Ritz-Carlton hotels. Fulfill hotel guests' wishes, both spoken and implied.*

2. *Use the power the company provides to create memorable guest experiences.*

3. *Become part of the company's charitable activities, its hospitality and its "mystique."*

4. *Look for ways to make the hotel and its service even better.*

5. *Assume immediate personal accountability for fixing guests' problems.*

6. *Work with colleagues as team members to meet each other's needs and serve guest.*

7. *Capitalize on any chance to learn more and develop professionally.*

8. *Become involved in planning their job's scope and responsibilities.*

9. *Take pride in how they look, act and speak.*

10. *Protect guests' and other employees' private information; be aware of their security.*

11. *Maintain facilities that are safe, accident-free and sparkling clean.*

I love Ritz Carlton's core values #'s seven and eight. They especially resonate with me because many of my coaching clients do not perceive this as a core value in their current companies. These clients are seeking coaching to find a new job and develop a transition plan to become part of a company that values them as people.

As you are continuing your *Project of You Plan* research, make learning the core values of any institution that you plan to attend or organization that you may want to work with, part of your process. Refer to your core values and consider if you feel this would be a good match. Document what you have learned for future reference using the Core Values Research worksheet.

Download the **Core Values Research Worksheet** from my website: www.marchforwardconsulting.com or utilize the **Core Values Research Worksheet** in **The Project of You Workbook.**

As you march forward in your life beyond high school, this research is a great habit to develop to learn more about a future connection before committing.

LET'S GET REAL WITH $

THERE ARE 2 major considerations as far as money is concerned at this point in your life.

1. What do you need to make salary-wise to be happy?

2. How much educational debt are you willing to take on to reach your goals?

When you are planning any project, you need to start with the outcome. Remember the most important project you will ever work on is you so start there with what you want.

First, what are your personal desires and what type of lifestyle/economic status do you need to be happy? Is it important to you to have a big house? Luxury car? Take five star vacations? Wear expensive designer clothes? There is no judgment here; it's what matters to you and there is no right or wrong. Consider what you want in your life and add up the numbers to discover what you need to make to "be happy and self-supporting".

If your parents and guardians are independently wealthy and planning to support you indefinitely, you can skip this chapter. Lucky you!

Either way, you have to consider this as you move ahead but proceed with caution. Don't fully give up on your dreams just because they may not be as lucrative as something else that you can choose.

Once you have a general sense of the lifestyle you want, begin to consider how you will get there. Do the research needed to have a general understanding of the potential salaries in your areas of interest, and consider this as you move ahead and make your plans.

Download the **My Budget and Salary Range Worksheet** from my website: www.marchforwardconsulting.com or utilize the **My Budget and Salary Range Worksheet** in **The Project of You Workbook.**

This is not an exact science as opportunities and salaries are in constant flux and can be unique to an individual. Consider questions like: How hard are you willing to work? Will you develop a side business and have an additional revenue stream? But having a general idea of the possibilities in your area of interest will give you a starting point for your plan.

The second component to consider is the amount of debt that you might potentially incur by completing your college Bachelor's degree as well as potentially completing a Masters degree and a PhD.

Again, if your parents and guardians are independently wealthy or have been great savers and planning to pay for whichever college options you choose, you can skip this chapter. Lucky you!

Or if you have a talent that will get you a scholarship, again lucky you and congratulations on your hard work. You can skip part two of this chapter.

While a specific college or technical school may be appealing to you, if the annual tuition of the college or technical school you choose is greater than your potential annual salary, an experienced accountant would not feel it is a good investment, especially if you are paying by taking out student loans. Your debt to potential earnings ratio is an important assessment to make before making your final plan. Looking at your potential budget and weighing what you really want, is a key component to find the best fit for you to march forward beyond high school and become what I refer to as HHSS – healthy, happy and self-supporting. If your student loans are overwhelming, it is hard to be happy and self-supporting and this creates stress for you, causing you to not feel healthy either. Gaining a general understanding about personal finance and budgeting is essential to transitioning beyond high school.

I would recommend that you take the time to read:

Too Smart for the Ivy League: How to Give Your Kids the Best College Education for the Least Amount of Money by Ms Jamie Dickenson

Jamie is a friend and colleague and has many great ideas and experiences related to considering the financial side of college planning.

Or if you would prefer to take a quicker, shorter path, I have an experienced accountant who works with March Forward Consulting and meets with students and young professionals to help them establish a budget and financial plan. You can have your parents or guardians accompany you for your financial planning session. If you use a MarchForwardConsulting Beyond High School Planning package, a financial session is included or it can be booked separately.

Finding the right career and the right school for you and spending the least money can be easier if you do the self-exploration and develop your plan before selecting your college. Getting real about the costs and possible debt accrued in your Beyond High School Plan and your potential salary is an important part of the process. This is the last step so don't focus on the costs before you have an idea who you are, what you want to do, and make your *Project of You Plan.*

THE THING ABOUT PASSION

WHAT IS PASSION? Passion is defined as a strong feeling of enthusiasm or excitement for something or about doing some specific activity. I believe my passions are the things that will make me feel sheer joy.

You can have more than one passion and it doesn't have to be your career. Many people are passionate about many things and they are such a pleasure to be around. If you connect with your passion(s) and embrace them, there are always new things to learn and enjoy. If you love travel, music, fitness, discovering new foods, technology, law, art, literature, or any other subject, it will fulfill your time and energy and help you stay focused and positive. Work hard every day at something that matters to you.

Your work might be one of your passions. I want to clarify my definition. First, yes you can potentially have more than one passion. You can have many passions. And second, it can be anything. The list is endless and varied. Your passion doesn't necessarily have to be how you support yourself. If you have discovered your passion and you have also found a way to make a living with it, you are one of the lucky ones. It can serve you for many years. Don't allow yourself to give your passion up just because you "grew up".

Your passion(s) may be the most important part of you. How you live out your passion is as unique as your DNA. And whatever your passion is, it ignites those around you and your larger community in a positive way. Imagine a pile of leaves, twigs, and logs without a flame; there would never be a fire. We are all fire starters once we have found our match. We are all meaning making machines!

My hope for you is that you find both things that you are passionate about that you do simply for the pleasure of the activity as well as an eventual career that connects to your gifts and gives you a sense of purpose. If you are lucky enough to be passionate about both in your Beyond High School Plan as far as advanced schooling and your career choice, you will be driven and successful. And if you have another passion like my friend Claire who loves music and is taking drum lessons just for fun, don't stop because you "grow up". No one makes Claire do that and she doesn't get a grade, a paycheck or something to add to her resume by practicing the drums, but she is passionate about music. Or recall Kayla who was passionate about art but told that she couldn't make a living as an artist until she learned about a career as a graphic designer. I have spoken to numerous students who loved painting or singing or acting or basketball or debate or any other activity that they were involved in during high school. Many feel that they don't have time beyond high school or they need to grow up and focus on grades or career and should be "more serious and committed". Never give up your passion(s); it fuels your positive energy.

I have had several young clients who were passionate about music and good at either singing or playing an instrument. Their parents discouraged them from choosing this as a career path, saying that they could not possibly support themselves that way. While I thought these parents were discouraging these children's dream, I have since reconsidered that position.

I was speaking with a local musician, Andrew Lipke, at a house concert. Andrew shared a new insight for me. He makes his living as a musician and he said your parents are the first gatekeepers. You will receive many rejections as a musician and if you can't overcome your first objection from your parents, then you won't make it. In other words, if you truly believe it is your passion and your mission, go for it. It takes dedication and commitment to make it in any field but some careers such as music, writing, theatre, and other arts are more difficult to find a way to support yourself.

Even if you don't find a way to support yourself playing music, writing poetry, drawing, painting, or any other activity that you feel passionate about, don't stop enjoying it just because you are an adult. I've coached many adults who have become re-energized in their lives by re-connecting to their passions that they let go after high school or college.

Success is liking yourself, liking what you do, and liking how you do it.

~ Maya Angelou

HELPING OTHERS BRINGS YOU JOY

DO YOU LOVE helping others find success? Have you experienced the joy that helping others provides? You have heard the quote, "you have to put on your mask before you can assist others". Always take care of you first, find your way, develop your plan and stick to it, as long as it's still working for you. But don't be afraid to try the road less traveled. Helping others with something you are passionate about will help you learn and grow and find new power in yourself.

Establish your sense of satisfaction, contentment, fulfillment, passion, or purpose in your world by becoming my mantra for you: HHSS – Happy, healthy and self-supporting. But also consider how you can give back and help others reach their own HHSS status. Consider volunteering or starting something that matters.

Blake Mycoskie who started Tom's Shoes wrote a book called, *Start Something That Matters*. I highly recommend your reading it if you have a desire to make a difference in the world. It is extremely inspirational and full of new ideas about starting new businesses, non-profits, or an exciting new project.

This book is for you, *"if you are curious about how someone who never made a pair of shoes, attended fashion school, or worked in retail created one of the fastest-growing footwear companies in the world by giving shoes away"*. (taken from the back cover of Blake's book.)

I have found with all of my clients that helping others truly does bring them joy. In some cases, you may feel overwhelmed or unhappy

with your life but when you focus on helping someone else, it can

change your mindset and bring you joy. The concept of helping oth-

ers to bring you joy is applicable in all areas of your life, whether in

high school, college, or your career. Helping and empowering others

will add to your success and cause you to feel joy.

"As we look ahead into the next century, leaders will be

those who empower others."

~ Bill Gates

YOUR BIGGEST FANS

"Life is not about finding yourself.
Life is about creating yourself."
~ Lolly Daskal

IN MOST CASES your biggest fans are your parents and guardians and they are wonderful! I am a parent myself and I can tell you that my three children are the most amazing young adults on the planet.

Your parents and guardians will always be there, and I'm not saying that you shouldn't count on them but be cautious. Know that they will generally always be your biggest fans and that is how it is supposed to work.

Consider if you were a famous entertainer or athlete. Who are you trying to please? Your fans. Your fans are the people who would buy your records or watch your movies or buy T-shirts with your name on it. We all want people who build us up and encourage and praise us. Many of the students that I work with want to please their parents and guardians. This is a normal feeling. But if you are developing your plan to please them and not being true to yourself, that is not a good situation. Remember Nate who majored in accounting because his biggest fans, his parents, told him that was the best path for him. Instead of connecting to his vision of wanting to develop computer games, he tried to please them and ended up dropping out of college. Or think

194

about Ryan, who decided what was right for him and changed schools after his first year against his parents' advice. He knew what was best for him even though it was a tough decision.

Learn to enjoy your biggest fans and share with them confidently as you learn more about who you are, even if it is not necessarily what they are recommending for you. You are the one who has to find your path to become HHSS; remember that is the end goal. Listen to your biggest fans and enjoy their unconditional support. It is a gift. Thank them for all that they do but remember as you learned at the beginning of this book, "it's all up to you".

ENRICH YOUR LIFE WITH
YOUR PASSION(S)

HOW MANY OF you know the song "Don't Stop Believing" by Journey? It encourages you to never give up on your dreams, passion, and loves.

Don't stop believin' Hold on to that feelin'

I believe that staying connected to your passion(s) will prolong your life.

Believing in yourself means believing in your passions!

In many cases, passions can be handed down through generations of families. I was lucky. My parents gifted me with the passion for music, and gave us opportunities to develop many passions. I believe that my strongest passion is for music of any kind. As a child my mother would burst into song whenever a line or word sparked a connection to a song she knew. So when we were getting our snow boots on, she sang and we learned Nancy Sinatra's "These Boots are made for walking, and that's just what they'll do, one of these days these boots are gonna walk all over you!"

Funny, many years later in 2009, I had a moment of sheer joy thanks to my knowledge of those words. I won a "finish that lyric contest" on a cruise with my family there to watch me in my favorite LBD and a good hair day to boot…what a great moment. Life is full of sweet surprises when you live your passion!

So how did my mother have such a passion for music?

My passion may have started further back in my family. I'd like to tell you a little about my Granny, my mother's mother and how her passion prolonged her life.

My Granny was a special person, someone I could learn so much from, but I didn't always understand that. I was fortunate; I had her in my life for a long time. You would be pretty amazed if you knew all she had been through in her life - many tough situations. Her life was what we in our generation would consider hard times. Granny was a wise, loving, compassionate, hard-working woman and she taught me many important lessons. The most important lessons were to live in the present moment and not fear the future and live your passions.

When I was young, I couldn't imagine her life, living on a farm. As time went by and her physical health declined, she went to live in a nursing home. As I got older and matured, I had begun to realize what an incredible gift it was to have her in my life. Many people don't even know their grandparents.

There is one extremely valuable lesson that she taught me indirectly that I would like to share with all of you. She loved music and especially loved listening to gospel music. She and my mother often just belt into a song with the slightest encouragement or as Forrest Gump would say, for no particular reason at all. Granny made the most of her time at the nursing home and was an integral and uplifting part of the community there. She was generally the leader of the singing activities there.

At 95, Granny announced that she planned to live to be 100 years old. Didn't sound too crazy at that point? Only 5 years to go right?

Sadly at 97, she developed a tumor. The only solution for her then to be able to live a life outside a hospital bed would require surgery. The doctors caring for her felt she was too old and fragile to survive surgery so they had decided to only provide her palliative care. One night when I went to visit her, sadly assuming it might be one of the last times that I would see her, an amazing thing happened. It was what many would likely refer to as a "perfect storm". The doctor in charge of her care was there and the occupational/music therapist from the nursing home stopped in to see her. She came in with all her positive energy and singsong attitude and asked, "Dorothy, when are you getting out of here? We need you back at the home in time to lead the Christmas Carols?" My Granny answered that she hoped soon because she wouldn't want to miss the Christmas caroling season. She liked singing and she liked being in charge; I don't wonder where I get that either. There was a moment of silence in the room for the elephant that had just walked in again at that moment.

We all quickly looked around and you could see the doctor's internal wheels turning as she pondered what she had just heard. Within seconds the doctor asked to speak to my mother outside. She stated that it was not her place to play GOD. Who was she to consciously remove their Christmas Carol leader? And that if my grandmother wanted the surgery, who was she to tell her no. They weighed the options and realized that her life wasn't working as it stood. The doctor then asked my Granny what she wanted. And she said that she felt comfortable letting the good lord decide. If she died on the table, so be it. It was out of her hands but staying in a hospital bed was not an option she wanted to pick.

They did the surgery, it was s success, and she was back in the home in time to lead the Christmas carols. I made sure to be there for them to make time to rejoice with her. I loved seeing the 'smiling eyes' of the singers as they rejoiced in song and the Christmas spirit!

My Granny lived three more years and passed away comfortably in her sleep,

3 months and 6 days after her 100th birthday. There was a huge celebration and recognition of her 100th birthday and she was still 100% clear headed at the event.

My Granny's choice to live her passions, music and her strong faith prolonged her life and allowed her to live to her 100th year! My Granny did not live in fear; she lived with passion, faith and compassion. She took each day as it came to her.

So never give up your passions, they may one day prolong your life!

Moving from High School to Beyond

As you are moving from high school, where your parents and guardians, teachers and coaches often hold you accountable, you have a myriad of choices of how to live your life. You are no longer locked into the predictable schedule and expectations that are part of the typical high school experience.

As the saying goes, "The world is your oyster", and I hope that you make the most of it. While there is an endless list of inspirational quotes and life lessons available, I listened to Dr. Oz deliver this list at the WCU graduation 5/7/2011.

I couldn't have written a better list so why re-invent the wheel.

While it was targeted at college graduates, I believe it's appropriate as an inspiration for high school students preparing for beyond high school also.

Print it out and post it somewhere; you will see it as a daily reminder of the possibilities in your life.

Ten tips I wish I knew when I graduated from college:

10. Everyday, feel productive and challenged in a tailor-made system that works for you, what works in your life. You might as well do the things you are good at.

9. Generate an expertise in an area other than the profession that you choose to make your living.

8. Develop a system for living your life.

7. Find a mentor.

6. Whatever you choose to do, do it with a childlike passion.

5. Let people surprise you.

4. Recognize that relationships have to keep growing, reinvent yourself at least every 7 years.

3. Never forget that the body is the temple of the soul.

2. Live in the present.

1. Remember that you must make the driving force in your life, love.

Getting to truly know yourself is a gift that you want to start working on as soon as you sincerely realize that

1. you have choices and

2. what you make of your life is truly up to you ,

so that the most important project you will ever work on is You!

Ask yourself again:

What project could you possibly be working on that is more important than understanding you and deciding what's next for you beyond high school?

Your parents, teachers, coaches, mentors and other supporters are wonderful people that are great resources, but they are peripheral to you becoming the amazing person that you choose to become in your adult life.

Now that you have completed this Values key skills section, do you feel like you have more clarity about how you can potentially negotiate your path towards a career, college, or whatever option you choose beyond high school?

Have you:

1. Recognized your core values?

2. Researched connecting to others' Core Values?

3. Analyzed your budget to Get Real with $?

4. Connected to your passions?

5. Decided how you will help others?

If you cannot answer YES to all the questions above, go back and complete the unfinished exercises.

If you can answer all these questions with a YES, you are ready to march forward and live your Project of You Beyond High School Plan.

YOUR PROJECT OF YOU PLAN
MARCHING FORWARD

NOW THAT YOU have completed all five key skills for success sections:

- Time,

- Self – awareness

- Connections

- Communication and

- Core Values

you are ready to negotiate your path towards a career, college, technical school, or whatever option you choose beyond high school.

Keep researching, exploring, experiencing and learning about you and the larger world beyond your high school. Even though I have written this book, I believe that research and experience is what you need to develop your the *Project of You Plan*. I have had many clients of all ages who have read books to figure out what they want to do. The answer is not in a book. It's inside you and is ignited by putting in the time to become self aware, make the connections, ask the questions, gain experience, and acknowledge your core values.

Have you:

1. Learned to prioritize your time and goal setting?

2. Increased your self awareness?

3. Discovered your connection?

4. Practiced and honed your communication success skills?

5. Recognized your core values?

6. Developed your *Project of YOU Beyond High School Plan?*

If you cannot answer YES to all the questions above, go back and complete the unfinished exercises.

The last step in your *Project of You Plan* is to complete your "Project of You Ongoing Plan Worksheet".

Download **the Project of You Ongoing Plan Worksheet** from my website: www.marchforwardconsulting.com or use **the Project of You Ongoing Plan Worksheet** in **The Project of You Workbook.**

Develop your next steps to keep marching forward and remember:

- Maintain the habit of investing time in your *Project of You Plan* by setting weekly goals and working with an accountability partner.

- Change is constant so as you continue to learn more about who you are and what you want, update your plan accordingly.

- Keep up with your research and dig deeper to make new connections and strengthen current relationships.

- Practice and improve on your success communication skills.

- Continue utilizing your core values to anchor your life plans and goal development.